Every Woman Should Go to Law School

OR READ THIS BOOK

Every Woman Should Go to Law School

OR READ THIS BOOK

MARGARET BASCH, J.D.

HarperResource

An Imprint of HarperCollins*Publishers*

This book is designed to provide accurate and authoritative information in regard to the subject matter covered. It is sold with the understanding that the publisher is not engaged in rendering legal, accounting, or other professional services. If legal advice or other expert assistance is required, the services of an attorney or other competent person should be sought. While every attempt has been made to provide accurate information, neither the author nor the publisher can be held accountable for any error or omission.

HarperCollins books may be purchased for educational, business, or sales promotional use. For information please write: Special Markets Department, HarperCollins Publishers Inc., 10 East 53rd Street, New York, NY 10022.

FIRST EDITION

Designed by Elliott Beard

Library of Congress Cataloging-in-Publication Data has been applied for.

ISBN 0-06-095360-8

00 01 02 03 04 ❖/RRD 10 9 8 7 6 5 4 3 2 1

For every mom who struggled to pave the way for her daughters. Especially my own.

Contents

Acknowledgments

My clients for their patience. Rick and Clara. Judges Fink and Boharic. Congressman John Porter's office. Representative Carol Krause. The reference staff at the Arlington Heights, Illinois, library. Jerry Ratigan. Inspector K. Carol and Ann. Tracey and Lisa. Chris "the voice of Eau Claire" Krok. Every person who must remain nameless but who contributed an anecdote. Lou and Tom. Skipp. Ken M. Karen. My friends at HarperCollins. . . Gail, Mauro, Susan, Lia, Andrea, Betsey, and most of all, Bridget Sweeney.

Thanks, most of all, to everyone who buys this book. (But remember, compared to law school, it's a bargain.)

Introduction

Law school is a means to an end. Without the piece of paper (*juris* doctor degree), and the cool hood you wear (but can't keep) at graduation from law school, you can't take the bar exam. Without taking (and passing) the bar exam you can't be an attorney. To be an attorney is to have power. People open my mail simply because the envelope says "Law Offices" in the upper left-hand corner. People take my calls because I introduce myself as "*Attorney* Margaret Basch." So for these reasons alone every woman should go to law school. Having a law degree is like having a magic wand.

The most valuable lessons I've learned were taught *after* graduating from law school, during my years practicing law. And those are the lessons I want to teach you. Although learning these principles will not make you a lawyer, they will make you into someone people listen to and respect. They'll get your foot in the door to wherever it is that you want to go. People will pay *attention* to your needs, and you will have the *resources* to have your needs met.

Many women find themselves in situations that could greatly improve if they only knew a few of the things that all lawyers know. Let me share a story that illustrates this notion. I accidentally took one of those "new age" continuing education classes at our local high school. The topic was something about relationships, so, of course, the class was made up entirely of women. The second night, I sat next to an elderly, almost frail, woman whose eyes were red and puffy from crying. Her house had sustained some rain damage. She hired a contractor who agreed to do the necessary repairs and who promised to charge her only what the insurance company had agreed to pay. After the work was done the contractor told her that the project was more involved than he originally thought. Now, he said, she owed him an extra two thousand dollars! She was completely distraught trying to figure out how to come up with the extra money.

This may sound terrible, but all I could think at that moment was, "Thank God I'm a lawyer." I was once in a similar situation. When I bought my first house, I hired a contractor to do some remodeling work. I agreed to pay him $5,000, total, with $2,000 up-front. I gave him the deposit, and would you believe I never saw him again! Well, I finally did see him—in court! He took my $2,000 and didn't do a minute of work. Yes, he knew I was a lawyer, and yes, I sued him. He met me on the courthouse steps on the court date and gave me my money back, plus court costs, all in cash. Was it a pain in the butt to have to sue him? You betcha. Did I cry and get red and puffy-faced and wring my hands? No way. Because unlike the little old lady in my new-age relationship class, I knew I had options beyond crying.

The purpose of this book is to *empower* women so they can make the most of all the opportunities that come their way. For the short run, I'll teach you how to draft a lawsuit, write an action letter, draft a will, use a law library, and more. For the long run, I'll share how to build enough confidence to handle a bully, set up a useful network of people and then use it, bring in business, and enjoy great success in any chosen field. I'm glad to share the resources I've discovered and developed from practicing law and working within a system that doesn't always give women the power they deserve and are entitled to.

So why is this book only for women? Because despite the great strides women have made in recent generations, it's still in too many ways a man's world. Women now have opportunities that our mothers never had, but we must still play by the *old* rules. Men made the rules of the game before we women were allowed to play. Then they passed on the rules and the nuances of the game from father to son.

Shake hands. Be prompt. Delegate authority. These are some of the "basics" that men have learned from their fathers and mentors. Women never had power, to speak of, until recently.

So, not only could women not pass on these rules from mother to daughter, thanks to the fellas we had far fewer opportunities to be mentored by knowledgeable people. And many of the rules we did learn from other women are suitable only in domestic situations, and prove useless in the worlds of business, politics, and commerce. So aside from the practical applications that the law offers, the world of law school and lawyering offers a place to learn these rules because it's still a male-dominated field. For example, in Illinois, where I practice, half of the current law school grads are women, but fewer than ten percent of the board of trial lawyers are women, *even now*. This is better than the *two* women who were on the board (there are eight now) when I started practicing, but it's still not good.

Unfortunately, every woman can't possibly go to law school, but they *can* read this book and then start making the rules, lessons, and principles of lawyers work for them.

1

Power!

(THE BASICS)

Power enables women to make the most of the opportunities now available to them. So, what is power? Whether we're talking about individuals or corporations, states or entire nations, power is the ability to affect others. But while the *essence* of power is the same, its ramifications vary depending on the situation and the size of the entities involved.

The amount of power in the universe—or at least, in the universe as we know it—is *finite*. If a person or a group or a country gains power, then another must necessarily lose power. There is only so much to go around. If my law firm gains market share, we take business another firm might have had. When I win a motion in court, another lawyer loses. If a colleague belittles me, and I refuse to accept his behavior, he loses power over me.

Women seem to understand this concept innately, whereas men will fight you on it. For example, if one male and one female coworker are friends and work well together and they both come up for a promotion, the woman will worry how her friend will feel if she gets the promotion: Is she really more qualified? Will he resent it when he has to answer to her? Will she be getting more than her share of power?

What about the man? He just wants the promotion. The only thing he'll worry about is what kind of tie he should wear on his first day as VP.

To test my theory about how men and women each think about power, ask them this question: If you gain power, does someone else have to lose it? Women will think about it first, and then most likely answer "yes." Men won't bother thinking. They'll just say, "No," because it doesn't matter to them. Their consciences don't bother them when their power was gained at someone else's expense.

Men want as much power as they can get and the repercussions of getting it simply don't occur to them. The moral of the story is, if it's power you want, then you'll have to go out and seize it and stop worrying about the effect it will have when you do. No one is going to hand power to you for free, and certainly no one is going to voluntarily part with his share.

The only man I know who is willing to acknowledge that power is finite is Michael Korda, who wrote the book *Power*. Korda, quoting Frederick Meinecke, surmises that, "Whoever fails to increase his power, must decrease it, if others increase theirs." I recommend Korda's *Power* heartily.

Each relationship involves a balance of power that is always in flux. You may willingly relinquish some of your power, and this is not a bad thing, *especially if it is your decision to share it*. For example, if you tell your husband that he can pick the spot of your next vacation, you have relinquished some of your power. Gaining power is not always good and giving up power is not always bad, but we should understand the power dynamic if we are going to play the game of life effectively. Truly powerful people know that giving certain kinds of power over to others actually builds more power for the giver!

So, power can be had by moving up the corporate ladder, or getting elected to Congress, or winning an important award— but it can also be gained by getting your previously uncooperative family to pick up after itself, by having friends who will help you out in a pinch no matter what your current status at work happens to be, or by not sacrificing your dignity for your boss. However, power will remain elusive without mastering a few basics first. We'll start with these.

Shy? Get Over It!

Remember the first grade—the little brown-eyed girl with the pixie haircut and the frilly dress hiding behind the teacher during recess? That was me. My memories of childhood pretty much involve: a) hiding behind my mother's skirt when my mother was around to hide behind, or b) getting bullied whenever she was not. People who know me now find this hard to believe, but I was painfully shy until about a year after I graduated law school.

Desperate friends and family tried to help me. My dad enrolled me in acting classes when I was a kid in a vain attempt to help me overcome my shyness or at least to get me to speak louder than a whisper. In high school, my guidance counselor diagnosed me with "low self-esteem." His assessment could not have been further from the truth. If anything, I had delusions of grandeur. I knew I was smart. I had certain talents, but I wasn't the cheerleader type. All through college, I was pretty much a straight-A student, but only my teachers knew it. I doubt you could find a classmate who even remembers my name. I never even raised my hand to participate.

Law school was no different. You know the ban against prayer in school? Thank goodness no one will ever be able to ban silent prayer, because I got through law school saying one prayer over and over again: *"Please, God, don't let him call on me."*

Are you getting the picture? I was terribly, painfully shy. Thank goodness we grow as we age. I needed to make a living after law school and I realized shyness could control my life. I could not make a living and stay shy. So, through practice and patience with myself, I overcame my shyness and became assertive. I'm still a nice person, but I'm not a doormat.

I changed my life, first in baby steps, then in leaps and bounds. Every woman controls her life. No woman should be battered, emotionally or physically, at home or at work. Too many women accept the status quo.

We control our own fates to a greater extent than we are willing to take responsibility—or credit—for. If *you* sail your ship into a storm, is it the storm's fault when your boat sinks? If *you* surround yourself with incompetent workers, is it their fault if a job doesn't get done right? If *you* make friends with miserable people, is it their fault that your weekends are torture? Think about it. It may seem easy to cast blame elsewhere when your life isn't going the way you had hoped. Actually life is easier when you take responsibility and control of your life. Your personal power increases tremendously. Power is good.

Conquer the Shyness Monster

I have met very few people in my life who don't admit to at least a little shyness. A *very* little shyness can be a good thing. It is akin to humility, which is a virtue. Great trial lawyers get a little nervous when arguing to a jury. They worry that the jury won't like them and then punish their client for it. This is healthy and often makes these lawyers prudent and conscientious.

You need to strike a balance. Take the example of a new lawyer doing her first trial. If she is *too* nervous or shy, she may mumble. Her voice will quake. Her knees can shake. She may support herself behind a lectern and appear to be hiding from the jury. A jury may misinterpret this shyness as a lack of confidence in the client's case or as simple inability to do her job. Either way, the lawyer simply has too little confidence in her own ability to do her client's arguments justice—and the jury knows it.

The converse may also adversely affect a lawyer's presentation. Established lawyers, if they're not careful, can get lazy and even cocky. After a dozen or so trials, a lawyer is a veteran and he may think he needs no practice or preparation. If he is a renowned lawyer who has won big or important cases, he may think the jury is lucky to be in his presence at all. When this happens, a good jury will teach the lawyer otherwise.

Shyness in the right dose can be a good thing. The trick is to master our shyness to the point that it is noticeable only to ourselves.

How does one overcome shyness? For me it wasn't a matter of choice. I started my own law practice. Overcoming my shyness was literally the difference between eating and starving. Starting my own business was a very scary proposition for me. I didn't have a huge financial cushion, so I had to sink or swim pretty quickly. Since I started my practice in the same general community in which I grew up, lots of people knew me. Still, I had to get the word out that I was a lawyer now, in private practice.

My problem was complicated by the fact that I only wanted to handle certain kinds of cases. I'm a tort lawyer, which means I do injury and damage cases. I could have a thousand friends and I could let every one of them know I have a new law practice, and it would still be possible that not one of them would ever need a tort lawyer. In fact, in the early days, I had to do a little bit of everything while I set myself up, just to put food on the table. In the first year, I handled two divorces and two contract disputes and two of just about everything else, in addition to lots of wills and finally some personal injury cases.

I did as much as possible to promote myself without having to overcome my shyness. I put ads in the Yellow Pages and in local newspapers. I sent announcements to my friends and family. Still, I knew that I had to *get out and meet people*. I decided to start with a local Chamber of Commerce. I remember vividly my first few "mixers." I literally went and stood by the food. Sometimes I went over to the bar and got myself a drink. I hoped that standing next to the buffet would entice people to come and talk to *me*. Well, someone did ask me, "Where are the napkins?" I started thinking networking was a fallacy. Everyone in the group already seemed to know everyone else and they didn't seem interested in including me in their clique. I never once put my hand out and introduced myself to anyone. For all they knew, I was the catering supervisor, surveying the spread.

About six months after I joined the Chamber of Commerce, I joined a Rotary Club. The one I connected with was small, only about twenty-five members, so it wasn't too intimidating. Also, you have a sponsor at Rotary Clubs. I attended the first few meetings with my sponsor, who introduced me around. I was warmly accepted into the group. Funny thing about shy people: They are only shy around strangers. Shy people are not shy with their friends. Because my sponsor introduced me around, and then my fellow Rotarians took me under their wings and introduced me around some more, I was soon friends with everyone in my small Rotary Club, and I didn't have to be shy.

One of the principles of Rotary is that if you miss one of your own chapter's meetings, you have to "make it up" by going to another chapter's meeting. So I began to miss and "make up" meetings on purpose, just so I could force myself to meet new people. I would put out my hand and I would say, "Hi, I'm Margaret. I'm making up." I can't tell you how difficult this was for me at first. But I did it.

Never once in all the times that I introduced myself to a stranger at a Rotary meeting did he say, "So what?" or "Who cares?" or any number of awful things I imagined. And I never had to introduce myself twice. Once I introduced myself to a member of the group, I was introduced to the group. I only had to muster the courage to introduce myself to one person, which, in the scheme of things, is a baby step. The leaps were taken for me. Let's say I introduced myself to John. Here's what would happen:

"Hi, I'm Margaret. I'm making up." I put out my hand and he shakes it.

"Hi, I'm John. What club are you from?"

"Oh, I'm from Arlington Heights."

"Do you have a business in Arlington Heights?"

"No, actually, I live in Arlington Heights. My law practice is here, in Schaumburg."

"Oh, really? What kind of law do you practice?" By then other members of the club are trickling in. Then John does the introducing.

"Ken, meet Margaret from the Arlington Heights club. She's a lawyer here in Schaumburg."

I shake hands with Ken and then Ken asks, "What kind of law do you practice?" I tell him, and then Ken tells me what he does, and then he introduces me to more people until they know me and I know all of them.

Not only did joining Rotary and then "making up" meetings in new places help me control my shyness, it helped me build my business, too. Many of my clients have come from referrals from my friends at Rotary.

Each new person you meet is a baby step in the leap that is overcoming shyness. As you gain more confidence your shyness will bury itself inside of you. It never disappears completely, but it will not hold you back.

One last thing: If you see a stranger standing alone near the food at a party, don't assume it's the caterer. Introduce yourself. Take the first step. It will be an act of kindness. Do it for someone else, remembering the times you wished someone had done it for you.

Command an Audience: Learn to Speak in Public

Okay. You got your toes wet by getting involved, and then you waded in. The water was a little cold at first, but once you got used to it, it was kind of nice. After a while you are comfortable jumping right into the deep water. Wow! Look at those people jumping off the high board! Do you wish that were you? Don't you wish you could not just jump off the high diving board, but do a triple-somersault-pike? Then everyone would envy *you*.

Public speaking is a lot like jumping off the high dive. Some people would rather disappear. Actually, some polls show that people would actually prefer to die than speak in front of a group. Public speaking is a tool all powerful people know how to use. Doing it well means commanding attention, having your opinions considered, and getting your needs met. That's power.

Shy people who have mastered their shyness can be the best public speakers. Why? Because we want to be accepted. We want so badly to be accepted that we try especially hard to do a great job with our presentations. When I do a speech, I want everyone in the audience to go home and say, "Wow, I'm so glad I heard Margaret speak today." When I'm preparing a speech, I always ask myself how I can get my audience to go home feeling pleased.

Giving a great speech, the kind that stays with the audience, is the equivalent of a triple somersault dive—really. When you hear a powerful speech do you ever think, "I wish I could give a speech like that"? You can, you silly! And then people will be saying that about *you*!

Start speaking to a group of people who already know and like you. Speak to your own Rotary club or garden club or book group. Talk about something you know. In Rotary there is something called a "classification" talk. Each new member of a club spends fifteen minutes explaining what he does for a living. That's easy enough, right? Plus, your fellow club members are your friends. They already like you, and one speech, good or bad, isn't going to change that.

Another good place to practice public speaking is Toastmasters. There are Toastmasters clubs all over the country. They also have a web site: www.Toastmasters.org. With each speech you give, you will become more confident. You'll also receive constructive criticism from your fellow members, which you can use to improve. You can read every book in the library on public speaking, but you won't *be* a public speaker until you speak in public.

Look, I went from being painfully shy to being a person who loves to do public speaking. I was lucky. The first speech I ever gave in my life, outside of school, was my Rotary classification speech. Yes, I was nervous, but I considered my fellow Rotarians my friends, and I knew they were cheering for me. Your friends don't want to see you fall on your face. My Rotary friends made my first public speaking event a big success. Eventually, as I got more involved in Rotary and I started holding offices at the district level, I started speaking at other Rotary Clubs and at district events. Many of the strangers in the audiences became friends as a result. Oh, and by the way, my law practice kept growing, too.

While I was in the middle of Toastmasters, the unthinkable

happened. I was asked to give the commencement address at Harper College, a local junior college. The invitation said that I was chosen because I was a role model for young people. Of course, I was honored. The letter also said there would be 2,500 people in attendance, and a considerable honorarium would be paid. I was floored. I was not at all prepared to give a speech in front of 2,500 people! I turned right back into little shy Margie.

My friend Ed, a fire chief, talked me into it. He not only told me what a great opportunity it was, he also asked me to use the fee to start a camp for young burn victims. Who could say no to a charity for kids? Right then and there I decided to overcome my fear of public speaking. In fact, I did the speech, took the honorarium, and endorsed the check to the people starting the Burn Camp.

So, how did it go? It could not have gone better. They laughed in all the right places. They got teary-eyed in all the right places. Many of them came to me and my family at the reception afterward and told me how much the speech meant to them. The head of the college's speech department congratulated me on a great talk. The chairman of the board told me it was the best commencement address in the—relatively short, I admit—history of the college. Is it any wonder I became addicted to public speaking?

Even though I was a novice, the Harper College talk went well because I spoke from the heart. I figured if they chose me because I was a role model for young people, then I would talk about what my life is about. My theme was "Do good work." I said, "It is important to do good work and excel in our chosen professions. It's also important to make our communities and our world better, to make a difference in the lives of others." These were not just words to me. I was baring my soul, and they knew it. I closed by saying to the graduates, "Go out and make your dreams come true. And if you can, help make someone else's dreams come true, too." Always speak the truth and always speak from your heart and you will not only be well-received, you will have power—*for there is power in truth.*

And always remember that the audience *wants* you to succeed. You've been in an audience. How often have you finished lunch and then turned to hear the keynote speaker and thought, "Gee, I hope she falls on her face," or "I hope she puts me to sleep. I could use a good nap"? Audiences want to be entertained, enlightened, moved. They consider you worthy of their much-treasured time. If they didn't, they wouldn't be there. They're giving you their positive energy. Take it and use it to give them what they want: a great speech, a part of you.

Reputation Is Everything

Quick, what is the male equivalent of a bitch?

We all know men who are aggressive and they're often called strong, powerful, and complex, among other things. We also know women who are aggressive who are known as bitches. Why is that? Because women never had much power until recently, so if a woman has power, she's probably taken it from someone else. That behavior goes against the grain of conventional ideas of femininity; therefore, powerful women are frequently known as bitches. Of course, some women are bitches. Some men are, too. We probably all have a bitchy streak in us, but it's important to control this feature of our personalities just as we want to control our weepiness or moodiness. We want people to associate with us—to do business with us, to socialize with us, to love us, whatever the case may be. Remember that people who like you and trust you will want to associate with you.

Why is reputation so important? Because if people don't want to associate with you, then your power is by necessity nonexistent.

Liars lie and *cheaters cheat*. Count on it. If you know that a man cheats on his wife or cheats on his taxes, do not do business with him. Play the odds. He will cheat you, too. If he cheats on the person he's supposed to love above all others, what makes you think *you* will be immune to his cheating ways?

If a lawyer tells me he'll go into court to get a continuance, and then he goes in and takes a judgment against my client, do you think I will *ever* trust him again? Not on your life. Not only that, but I will tell every other lawyer I know, and then they won't trust him, either.

So if you want the power that comes from good, honest working relationships, keep your reputation good by being honest, hardworking, and dependable. If you make a mistake, fix it. Invest in your good name.

Get a Grip: Controlling Your Emotions

It's appropriate to cry during sad times or emotional moments, but it's not appropriate to cry at work—*ever*. Business is still a man's domain, and women who conquer it play by the guys' rules. Men have been taught to "take it like a man" from the time they were tots. So if your boss reprimands you, or you don't get the promotion you were expecting, or something else of a professional nature slaps you upside the head, *do not cry*. Or at least wait until you get home.

Women who cry at work—or otherwise show inappropriate emotion—will be labeled unprofessional and even hysterical. So what do you do if you are a crier? Make an "I am *not* going to cry" plan. Then use it next time you feel like crying. I suggest first going into the ladies' room and taking lots of deep breaths. Then, when you have some privacy, call your most trusted confidante and make a date when she'll be available to listen to you express your full disappointment or outrage or whatever. *After* work you can have a good cry—it will still make you feel better, but you will not be labeled a lunatic.

Learn to take criticism not "like a man," but like the grown-up that you are. Nobody *likes* to hear she screwed up or that she needs improvement. But we're all growing. Listen to criticism and then, in a calmer moment, evaluate it. You might learn something, or you might decide the criticism is unfounded. You can only think clearly *after* the need to cry or rage or act out has passed. So learn to deal with it. You'll be thought of more highly by others and you'll be proud of your own ability to handle obstacles.

Assert Yourself

Okay, we know that aggressive women are known as bitches. We also know that women who don't stand up for themselves are known as doormats. Nobody wants to be known as either one. What we want to be is assertive. We don't want to walk all over anybody, and we don't want to be walked all over ourselves.

The following scenario explains the differences among passive, aggressive, passive-aggressive, and assertive. You go to a restaurant and you order a steak medium rare. It comes back well done. What do you do?

If you eat the steak, even though the waitress offers you the chance to send it back, you are passive. You spend your life thinking, "I should have . . ." (You are a doormat.)

If you call the waitress over and scream at her that she is a stupid idiot who cannot tell the difference between medium rare and well done, then you are aggressive. (You might even be a bitch.)

If you eat the steak and then you don't leave a tip and you drive over the restaurant's flower bed, you are passive-aggressive. (You are a bitchy doormat.)

If you call the waitress over and explain that the steak is not quite right and ask for a new one, then you are assertive. (Assertive is what we should all strive to be.)

Be careful with these labels because they tend to stick. If you are known as a bitch, people will steer clear of you long after you mend your ways. Similarly, if you are known as a doormat, people will be miffed and offended if you don't lie down for them like you've done for everyone else.

The only way to master assertiveness techniques is to practice them. So get started. Nobody is going to give you power. Use your resources. Ask for what you want, and you just might get it. This applies to raises, contracts, refunds, a great steak, and everything else that's important in your life. Go out and GET what's important to YOU.

Grab the World by the Tail

I had never seen a mountain until I was in my twenties. I had never been outside the United States, either. I had never seen an opera. I had never eaten sushi or swum in an ocean. There were so many things I hadn't tried. I was a lawyer, but I had no life experience. I was book-smart and street-silly.

When I was twenty-five, I had a relationship broken and I felt sorry for myself. I decided I was not an interesting person to be around, and in retrospect, I was right. I had no hobbies or passions. I had nothing to talk about. Plus, I was afraid to try new things. If someone asked me to dance, I would say, "I don't dance." If someone offered to take me skiing or golfing, I would answer, "I simply couldn't." Finally, I realized I didn't do much of anything.

I took dancing lessons and golfing lessons and skiing lessons. I worried that more experienced dancers and golfers and skiers would laugh when I tripped over my own feet or missed the ball or fell on my tushy. No one laughed—or at least, I didn't hear them. I learned that they were beginners once, too, and they were as crummy as I was. With time, they got better, and I would, too. When I lift weights, I lift a lot of weight. I've been weight training since high school, and each year I am able to lift a little bit more. Do I laugh at women just starting at the health club, who can barely bench press just the bar? No way! When I started, I couldn't bench press ten pounds ten times. I am glad for women starting out. I hope they like it as much as I do.

Now I love to try new things. Last spring I took snowboarding lessons with my nine-year-old nephew. Of course he caught on quicker than I, but even he didn't laugh at me. He thought it was cool his old aunt would get on a snowboard and hurtle down a mountain.

I started traveling. When I was younger, I traveled on a shoestring. It was fun. My sister and I traveled together a lot, and we were always on an adventure. When things went wrong, like when I got off the train in Paris and the doors closed and the train left with my sister still on it, we just knew we'd have a funny story to tell.

I went to my first opera, and then a second. Then I bought a subscription to the opera. When my friend Tom started giving me Bulls tickets, I became a basketball fan. I got to see Michael Jordan and his teammates win six NBA Championships.

I have had so many good times because I got off my duff. My new policy is to *go*. If someone asks me to do *anything*, if I'm not already doing something, I'll go. I went to my first hockey game last year. I can't say it was the ballet, but it was fun. I'd go again.

Every new experience is a resource that helps us grow as individuals. From experience comes knowledge, and knowledge is power.

Like I said earlier, these are the bare-bones basics. Once you've mastered them, you can get out there. Go get 'em.

2

Ignorance of the Law Excuses No One

(HOW TO USE A LAW LIBRARY)

Ignorantia legis neminem excusat.
If you guessed that the chapter title is the English translation of the widely quoted Latin statement above, you are hereby an honorary lawyer, and entitled to keep reading, along with everyone else.

Now, think about what those words mean. Ignorance of the law excuses no one (sometimes expressed as "ignorance of the law is no excuse" or "defense"). But who, even in the "information age," in our literate American society, is *not* ignorant of the law? Even lawyers don't know all or even most of the laws. The day a lawyer takes the bar exam is the day she knows the most law of her life. There are many reasons for this, but the number one reason is that the laws are always changing. New bills are enacted into law by Congress. Old laws are interpreted or even thrown out by the courts. State legislatures and cities and towns and villages are passing laws on a daily basis. That is why law schools don't teach the law. The law is in a constant state of flux.

By the way, in case you are wondering how it is that law school graduates do not learn law in law school, but know it for the bar exam, note that there is a whole industry called Bar Review that teaches law school graduates the law that they didn't learn in law school. No, really. I am not making this up.

Law schools will tell you that they teach their students to "think like lawyers." Actually, they teach students how to look up what the law is. Herein lies the problem. If ignorance of the law is no excuse, shouldn't *everyone* have the resources to look up the law? How are we to know what our rights and obligations are, under the law? And why should ignorance of the law *not* be an excuse?

On the other hand, ignorance of *the facts* is a defense. So, if you bring a box of Cuban cigars into the United States illegally, and you are detained at the airport, do *not* say, "I didn't know it was illegal to bring in Cuban cigars." Instead, look shocked and exclaim, "I didn't know those cigars were Cuban!" because ignorance of the facts is a defense.

I can't possibly envision all the legal answers readers of this book will want to know now or need to know in the future. The most common legal problems are related to disagreements like landlord-tenant disputes, employment conflicts, or breaches of contract. Not earth-shattering matters, but important to the parties involved, nonetheless. The new millennium and Internet commerce will bring about legal disputes never before thought possible. Is a contract entered into by electronic mail across state lines binding? If so, which state's laws will apply? Or will federal law control these matters? Nobody knows all of the answers, but you *will* know how to look them up.

Believe it or not, I th[...]
course on "How to Use a La[...]
our high school district and to the[...]
any part of it. "A little knowledge is a[...]
mentality. Non-lawyers couldn't possibly[...]
jailhouse lawyer (better known as a convict[...]
he will double over in laughter—after he finishe[...]
appeal based on his research done at the priso[...]
Knowing how to use a law library is a valuable tool, as [...]
how to use an encyclopedia. And who doesn't know how to[...]
encyclopedia?

Law libraries are everywhere and almost always open to the
public. Law schools and most colleges have them. Courthouses
have them. Some local libraries have them. Their use is not
restricted to lawyers. While it's true that lawyers, judges, clerks,
and paralegals are the primary patrons of law libraries, you will be
most welcome there, too (unless you do something illegal while
you're there). I promise if you're persistent you will become pro-
ficient at using your law library. The skills you learn will stay with
you forever, and you'll find them incredibly valuable.

To prove it could be done, I taught a one-day seminar called
"How to Use a Law Library" to a support group for women with
cancer. The seminar was full. Because I could not teach the class
at our local library, I brought a mini–law library to the seminar.
We had statutes, cases, and digests. I gave the women sample
problems and showed them how each library resource could be
helpful. I told them to practice using the law library in town several times so their newfound legal research skills would "stick,"
and they would be able to call them up when they had real legal
questions. Quite a few of the women called me weeks later to say
they had used the library to look up answers to legal questions
and they had felt empowered, and they thanked me profusely.

y need to use
w. They are:
d by a legisla-
cular matters;
nce you know
h to do basic

CE OF THE LAW EXCUSES NO ONE

ied to teach a community education
w Library." I offered the course to
library directly. Neither wanted
dangerous thing" was their
look up the law.' Tell any
d criminal) this and
s writing his own
law library.
s knowing
use an

a search for the
you an overview
of the law _____ tatutes (rules) and
cases (opinions). Digests steer you _____ nt statute or case
book more quickly. Every state has its own legal digest. There are
also federal digests. The West Publishing company publishes a federal digest and many of the state digests, too. Ask the law librarian
to point out the Wisconsin digest or the federal digest. You'll
sound like you belong and the librarian will not look at you funny.

Every digest has a subject index, usually in several volumes,
either at the front or the back of the set of books. (A digest takes
up a whole book case.) Sometimes there will be more than one
edition of the digest (for example, *West's Illinois Digest Second*, and
West's Illinois Digest Third). Always start with the most recent
digest, which is the one with the largest ordinal number.

The index to the digest has an amazing number of subjects
listed, and you will almost always find a reference to yours. For
example, say your dog bit your neighbor and the neighbor threatens to sue. You vaguely remember something about a "one free
bite" rule, but you don't know if it's true, or if it applies to your
case. You would look in the index under dog bites, where you'd

probably be referred to "Animal Control," or there might actually be a section of laws just for dog bites in your state. The index will refer you to the section of the digest that applies. For example, the entry "dog bites" refers you to Animal Control, Section 35, *et seq.* Pull out the digest volume with the A's—they are arranged alphabetically—and look up Animal Control and start reading at Section 35. *Et seq.* just means "and following," so you would start reading at Section 35 until you found what you were looking for.

Since digests mostly reference cases (opinions) but also statutes (legislative acts), the section on dog bites will likely provide a list of cases decided by courts in your state (or in the case of federal digests, federal courts) in which dog bites are discussed. The digest gives a condensed version of the ruling in the case as interpreted by the editor of the digest. Digest entries are meant to lead you to the actual case, but digest entries are *not* the law. They are examples of how a law was interpreted in a particular instance. If you find an entry in a digest that seems relevant to your question, you must still must look up the related case. If a statute is referenced in a digest, you must look up the statute.

Cases

Looking up cases is really very easy. Cases are found in case-books, surprisingly enough. Casebooks are also called reporters, because they just report the law. Judges write decisions and case-books report them, word for word. Each decision is preceded by editorial comments on the case, similar to those found in digests. These are meant to help you find what you are looking for in the case, but these comments in the reporters are not the law. Do not quote these explanatory comments as the law, because they are only one editor's opinion of the court's decision, based on his reading. You must read the case yourself. If the case is long and has many issues, you can use the editorial comments in the reporter to find the section of the opinion you are looking for. Each comment (also called a headnote) is numbered. You will find the same numbers throughout the case. Find the headnote that you feel answers your question and then find the matching number in the court's opinion. They should correspond, and provide the answer to your question.

For example, *People v. Wallace*, which is included in this chapter, has SIX numbered headnotes. If, after reading the headnotes, you decide #3 is of most interest to you, you can go to page 690 of the decision, where you will find [3], which corresponds to the headnote. There you should find the section of the decision that will be of the most help to you.

Each case has facts, an issue—or issues—and a resolution, which is the court's answer to the issue before it. Rarely will you find a case with the exact same facts as the situation you are researching. Maybe your little poodle puppy nipped at the heels of the next-door neighbor and caused some scratches. The case you find may concern a Rottweiler taking a bite out of a mailman. *The facts are not the same, but the same law applies to both cases.* Law school teaches for three long years how to take similar facts and apply the same law. It is pretty basic stuff and requires only a little practice.

Now, how do you find a case? Let's say you find a reference to a case in a digest, or you have a citation to a case from a newspaper. It will look something like this: *Jones v. Doe*, 123 MD2d 401 (1st Dist, 1989). In the example given, *Jones v. Doe* is the name of the case. State casebooks contain only appellate court cases and supreme court cases. As a rule, Jones (the first name in the case) would be the appellant or the person who appealed, and Doe (the second name) would be the appellee or the person who won at the trial court level. For various reasons, the names of the parties are sometimes reversed. Sometimes the plaintiff's name comes first whether he is the appellant or not. I don't know why. I think some courts just like to keep the case name all the way through the process. The plaintiff is the party who initiated legal action, i.e., the person who sued the other party. The party who was sued is the Defendant. In the casebook, the decision will say James Jones, Plaintiff-Appellant, v. Susie Doe, Defendant-Appellee. That is how you know who is who.

In the example 123 Md2d 401 (1st Dist, 1989), *123* is the volume number and *401* is the page number. *Md2d* is a reference to Maryland casebook, second edition. So, you would find the Maryland casebooks (reporters), look for "2d" on the binding, and find volume 123. The case *Jones v. Doe* would be on page 401. The information after the case name and number, in parentheses, is the district number of the court that issued the opinion, and the year the decision was handed down. What could be more simple? The headnotes will tell you the facts, issue, and decision in condensed form, and then the court's decision in whole will follow.

All of law school is spent reading cases. The average law student reads hundreds if not thousands of cases over the course of three years, even though the skill of reading cases is mastered after reading only a few. You, too, should be able to read cases with some fluency after studying just a few of them. They only *look* intimidating. Don't worry. Just remember the defendant is defending herself or her position, whether in a civil or a criminal case. In a criminal case, the government prosecutes the defendant, and in a civil case the plaintiff complains against the defendant. Plaintiffs usually claim that a defendant owes some monetary compensation for damages (for breach of contract, personal injury, etc.). If you come across a legal word you don't understand, look it up in a law dictionary. (*Black's Law Dictionary* will be in every law library and in most public libraries' reference sections.)

Statutes

Statutes are written rules. Congress passes a bill and it is signed by the President to become a federal statute. A state legislature passes a bill and it is signed by the governor to become a state statute. Unlike cases or digests, statutes won't include a judge's opinion, nor will they go into the details of a particular case. For our dog bite inquiry, for example, you might find a statute that says, "The owner of any dog that bites a person will be liable to that person for monetary compensation, regardless of whether the dog has been known to its owner to be vicious." And there you have it. That's the rule. There might be cases interpreting the statute. You find those in a digest. Some sets of statute books are "annotated," which means a minidigest is included. Each printed statute is followed by references to cases interpreting the statute. The annotations, while helpful, are not part of the statute.

You will find statute references in digests and in cases. You will also find them in the index to the statutes. Each state's statutes will also take up a bookcase, and the same is true of federal statutes. The index will be at the front or the back of the set. Just like with the digest, you look up the subject you are researching, like "dog bites" or "animal control," and you will be referred to certain statutes. Just like with cases, statutes are referenced by two numbers. The first number is the section of the statutes where you'll find it and the second will be a specific statute. 735 ILCS 411 means look up section 735 of the Illinois Compiled Statutes and find the statute number 411. Statutes are in numerical and not alphabetical order.

How do you know which statutes to use? Is it a state or a federal law? Could there be a local law? Because the U.S. Constitution reserves most lawmaking to the states, the state statutes are usually your best place to start. However, some things are exclusively or additionally covered by federal laws. Use of mails is one. Interstate commerce is another. Things like the Internet are starting to be regulated more often by the federal government because it would be impossible for a single state to control. If you're not sure, look in each set of statute books. Also, you might be able to get some direction from your state legislator or U.S. Congressman or local elected officials. See Chapter Four for more ideas.

And remember, even though statutes seem to be the most straightforward explanation of a rule or law, it's still important to see the various ways in which the rule may have been interpreted by the courts—which is why you should include casebooks and digests in your legal research.

Make Sure Your Law Is Current

Okay, you found a case or a statute that is right smack on point and answers your legal question. Congratulations, you're *almost* finished. Be aware the pocket part! Every digest book and every statute book has a little addition to it in the back "pocket." This is hard to describe, but you will see it at the library. It is literally a little pamphlet stuffed into the back of the book. Pocket parts are updated with much more frequency than the books them- selves and are filled with the latest available information and updates. After you find an appropriate digest section or statute in a book, check the same section in the pocket part to make sure the law in the book is still current. This sounds complicated, but it actually only takes a minute or two and is worth the effort; it might save you some embarrassment if it keeps you from quoting last year's law.

Digests and their pocket parts should lead you to current cases, but if you find a case that answers your legal question and you want to check to make sure no other case has superseded your case, you can check something called *Shepard's*, which is like a pocket part of cases, but is published by Shepard's Publishing. *Shepard's* are separate volumes from the casebooks. They have red covers and there are sets for federal cases and state cases. You look up your case citation (like 123 Md2d 401), and it will list more recent cases that have referenced your case, if there are any. *Shepard's* has a coding system that is listed in the front of every book so that you can find out with one quick glance whether newer cases follow the rule of law in the original case, explain it, or differ from it. Again, it can be confusing the first time you use it, but by the second and third times, you'll be a pro.

The Intimidation Factor

Some law libraries are bigger and more intimidating than others. Some local libraries have only federal and home state materials. Others have materials for every state, and then some. Don't worry. You don't have to deal with anything but the cases and statutes and digests for the state in which *you* have a problem—usually your home state, but sometimes (rarely) with the federal government. In addition to cases and statutes and digests, some libraries have other resources like law review articles and legal encyclopedias (these have names like *Corpus Juris Secundum* to deter you from reading them). Read them if you want to, but I doubt you will find them very interesting or useful. I have not cracked one open since law school.

Yes, a law library can be intimidating the first time you use one, or maybe the first few times. I guarantee if you take the time to practice using a law library, to look up real problems or imaginary ones just for the practice, you will begin feeling at ease. You will never know all the answers to every legal problem, but you will be able to locate the answers. Knowledge is power. Use yours wisely.

A Walk-Through

I've explained how to research a legal question. Now I will show you what your research will look like. First, we need a problem. Let's say you have decided to start a new business. It's going to be the greatest flower shop ever, and you decide to call your business "World's Greatest Flowers." You tell all your friends and they think it's a great idea, but one of them—the curmudgeonly one— says, "Well, I think that name is probably taken."

Hmmm, you think. "How can I find out?"

"Check Assumed Business Names," she tells you.

Not wanting to sound dumb (nobody ever wants to sound dumb), you resolve to look up this assumed name business at the law library. First, you look in the statute books (yes, you could look first in a digest, but order is not very important in legal research, and you should look both places). You would start in the index. On page 28, I have copied a page for you from the Illinois statutes index I found when I looked up "Assumed Names." See where it says "Assumed Business Name Act," one third of the way down the second column? I would start by looking up the statute number referenced there in the index.

And if I look up the statute, I find the Assumed Business Name Act, which tells me everything I ever wanted to know about assuming a business name and then some (see p. 29). Section One says (yes, I admit, in a convoluted legalistic manner) that before a person can conduct business under an assumed name (any name other than the person's legal name), she must register that name with the Clerk of the County in which she intends to transact her business. Section One also requires that the name of the business and the name of the owner be published in a newspaper that appears in the same county.

So now you know that you can't just throw up a neon sign that says "World's Greatest Flowers." You must register the business's

Index to compiled statutes.

NAMES AND RECORDS

ACT 405. ASSUMED BUSINESS NAME ACT

405/0.01. Short title

§ 0.01. Short title. This Act may be cited as the Assumed Business Name Act.

Laws 1941, vol. 1, p. 550, § 0.01, added by P.A. 86-1324. § 635, eff. Sept. 6, 1990.

Formerly Ill.Rev.Stat.1991, ch. 96, ¶ 3m.

Title of Act:

An Act in relation to the use of an assumed name in the conduct or transaction of business in this State. Approved July 17, 1941. Laws 1941, vol. 1, p. 550.

405/1. Necessity of certificate—Filing certificate

§ 1. No person or persons shall conduct or transact business in this State under an assumed name, or under any designation, name or style, corporate or otherwise, other than the real name or names of the individual or individuals conducting or transacting such business, unless such person or persons shall file in the office of the County Clerk of the County in which such person or persons conduct or transact or intend to conduct or transact such business, a certificate setting forth the name under which the business is, or is to be, conducted or transacted, and the true or real full name or names of the person or persons owning, conducting or transacting the same, with the post office address or addresses of such person or persons and every address where such business is, or is to be, conducted or transacted in the county. The certificate shall be executed and duly acknowledged by the person or persons so conducting or intending to conduct the business.

Notice of the filing of such certificate shall be published in a newspaper of general circulation published within the county in which the certificate is filed. Such notice shall be published once a week for 3 consecutive weeks. The first publication shall be within 15 days after the certificate is filed in the office of the County Clerk. Proof of publication shall be filed with the County Clerk within 50 days from the date of filing the certificate. Upon receiving proof of publication, the clerk shall issue a receipt to the person filing such certificate but no additional charge shall be assessed by the clerk for giving such receipt. Unless proof of publication is made to the clerk, the certificate of registration of the assumed name is void.

If any person changes his name or his residence address or the address of any place of business in the county where such assumed name is being employed after filing a certificate, or if the name of a person is added to any business organization for which a certificate is on file, such person shall file an additional, duly acknowledged certificate in the office of the County Clerk of the county in which such person transacts business under an assumed name. The certificate shall set out the change or addition as the case may be. Such certificate shall also set out the post office address of the person. If any business organization for which such certificate has been filed in any county of this State shall remove its place of business to another county in this State or shall establish an additional location for doing business in another county of this State, a certificate shall be filed in the office of the County Clerk of such other county and notice of the filing of such certificate of a change or addition of a name shall be published and proof of publication made pursuant to the provisions of this section in the same manner as is provided for original certificates to do business under an assumed name.

Laws 1941, vol. 1, p. 550, § 1. Amended by Laws 1945, p. 1088, § 1; Laws 1963, p. 2997, § 1; P.A. 76-892, § 1, eff. Aug. 20, 1969; P.A. 86-622, § 1, eff. Sept. 1, 1989.

Formerly Ill.Rev.Stat.1991, ch. 96, ¶ 4.

405/2. Change or addition of name— Certificate—Time for filing

§ 2. Persons conducting such business or any business under an assumed name who have prior to August 16, 1963 changed their names or whose names are additions to a business organization conducting business under an assumed name, for which a certificate has previously been filed, shall file another certificate setting out the change in their names or that their names are additions to a business already in operation and every address where such business is conducted or transacted in the county within 30 days after August 16, 1963.

References Are to Digest Topics and Key Numbers

ASSOCIATIONS AND SOCIETIES—Cont'd
JUDICIAL notice. **Evid 22**
JUROR—
  Disqualification of member. **Jury 88, 97(3)**
LABOR organizations, see, generally, this index Labor
  Organizations
LIABILITY of members—
  Acts and debts of association. **Assoc 16**
  Mutual liabilities. **Assoc 14**
LIBEL and slander. **Libel 10(5)**
MANDAMUS—
  Admission to membership. **Mand 124**
  Associations subject to mandamus. **Mand 122**
  Organization. **Mand 123**
  Reinstatement of member. **Mand 125**
MEDICAL and similar societies. **Phys 9**
MEMBERSHIP. **Assoc 6-11, 16**
  Liabilities—
    Acts and debts of the association. **Assoc 16**
    Dues, fines and assessments. **Assoc 12**
    Mutual. **Assoc 14**
  Rights. **Assoc 15**
MERGER. Consolidation or merger, generally, ante
MINING associations. **Mines 101**
MONOPOLIES—
  Business firm association, regulating member-
    competitor trade practices. **Monop 12(18)**
MOTORCYCLES, personal injuries, proximate cause, neg-
  ligence. **Autos 245(48, 59)**
MUTUAL benefit insurance associations. **Insurance 687-710**
MUTUAL ditch associations—
  Irrigation of lands of members. **Waters 238**
NAME. **Assoc 4**
NATURE of. **Assoc 1**
NEGLIGENCE. **Assoc 19**
NEWS associations. **Newsp 7**
OFFICERS. **Assoc 18**
  Foreign association—
    Service of process in Federal district court. **Fed Civ
      Proc 497**
  Libel or slander—
    Imputing unfitness, misconduct or criminal acts.
      Libel 10(5)
  Representation of the association. **Assoc 19**
ORGANIZATION. **Assoc 3**
PARTIES to actions. **Assoc 20(2, 3)**
  District Court of United States. **Fed Civ Proc 115**
PLEADING. **Assoc 20(5)**
POLITICAL parties. **Elections 121**
PROCESS. **Assoc 20(4)**
PROOF in actions by or against. **Assoc 20(5)**
PROPERTY. **Assoc 15**
RECEIVERS. **Assoc 21**
REINSTATEMENT of members. **Assoc 11**
  Mandamus to compel. **Mand 125**
REMOVAL of actions to Federal courts. **Rem of C 26**
REPORTS—
  Qualified privilege. **Libel 42(3)**
REPRESENTATIVE suits, by unincorporated associations.
  Assoc 20(2)
SEAL. **Assoc 4**
SERVICE of process. **Assoc 20(4)**
STATUS. **Assoc 1**
STATUTE of frauds—
  Creation of estates or interest in real property. **Frds St of
    56(9)**

ASSOCIATIONS AND SOCIETIES—Cont'd
STATUTORY provisions. **Assoc 2**
  Class legislation. **Const Law 208(4)**
  Special or local laws. **Statut 79(2)**
  Titles and provisions of laws. **Statut 113**
SUMMARY judgment. **Judgm 185.3(5)**
SURGEONS, expulsion after hearing, admission of act
  cited. **Const Law 318(2)**
SUSPENSION of member. **Assoc 10**
TAXATION. **Tax 112-171½**
  Income tax, see this index Income Tax
TORTS—
  Assoc 19
  Corp 491
TRADE unions, see, generally, this index Labor Organi-
  zations
TRADE-MARKS and trade-names, see this index Trade-
  Marks and Trade-Names
TRUSTEE or donee of charitable trust. **Char 20(1, 3-5)**
UNFAIR competition—
  Use of trade-marks and trade-names. **Trade Reg 493**
UNITED States courts, see Federal courts, ante
VENUE. **Assoc 20(1)**
  Issues and proof on plea of privilege. **Plead 111.16**
  United States courts. **Fed Cts 85**
  Weight and sufficiency of evidence. **Plead 111.42(6)**
WILLS—
  Devisee or legatee. **Wills 514-517**
  Identification—
    Evidence. **Wills 489(6)**
WITHDRAWAL of members. **Assoc 9**
WORKERS' compensation—
  Employees of workers' associations. **Work Comp 214**
ZONING regulations—
  Amendments or modifications, reasonableness. **Zon-
    ing 155**

ASSUMED OR FICTITIOUS NAMES

ABATEMENT and revival, suing in assumed name.
  Abate & R 21
ACCOMPLICES, withholding disclosure of present
  identities, danger to families. **Witn 267**
AFFIDAVIT for search warrant, quashing warrant and
  suppressing evidence seized under it—
    Crim Law 394.6(2)
    Searches 3.9
AUTOMOBILES—
  License or tax of persons doing business in fictitious
    name. **Autos 34**
  Title certificate, seller signing fictitious name. **Autos
    20**
BILLS and notes, payee in note unregistered fictitious
  name under which business conducted. **Bills & N
    32**
  Opening gas station for business, course of employ-
    ment. **Work Comp 1565**
BUSINESS under, statute making it unlawful to conduct,
  without certificate, constitutionality. **Names 10**
CHECK payable to fictitious person as payable to
  bearer. **Bills & N 6**
CHECK-KITING scheme, bank led to believe accused
  could be contacted by mail. **P O 35(8)**
COMPLAINT, signing with assumed name, validity of
  search warrant. **Searches 3.4**
COMPLAINT for search warrant. **Searches 3.6(3)**
CONDITION in will, assumption of name. **Wills 642**

name with your county clerk and publish the name with your own name in the newspaper. This is a good piece of information to have, and it directs you to your county clerk, who will be able to direct you further. Actually, the clerk's office will hold your hand and walk you through the process. They get registration requests every day and most people are applying for the first time, so the clerk will not think you are a moron for asking even the most basic questions. See Chapter Ten on getting the government to do your legal work for free.

Now, let's say you want to find out if there are any cases about assumed names, either for practice or because you have a question that is not answered by the statute. You would look in a digest. On page 30 is the first page of the index entry for Assumed Names in the digest. See that under Assumed or Fictitious Names there is an entry called Business, which refers to Names 10. This is part of a copyrighted system developed by the publisher of the digest (in this case, West Publishing) to organize areas of the law to make them easier to find. If you go to the volume with Names in it (they are arranged alphabetically, just like an encyclopedia), and find Section 10, it will provide references to court cases about assumed business names.

Here is what you find when you go to Names 10, shown on page 32. Several cases are listed on the first page (and the listing goes on for more pages). Let's say you want to read the case about the purpose of the assumed name statute—see *People v. Wallace*? All the numbers after the case name tell you where you can find the court's decision in that case. In this instance, it provides you with three different places to find it. The decision is the same in all three places, but most libraries will only have one of the three. In this case, the first reference, Ill. Dec. 687,397, is to Illinois Decisions; the second, N.E. 2d 20, 77, is to Northeast Reporter; and the third, Ill. App. 3d 979, to Illinois Appellate Decisions, which is the official reporter.

⊙══ **1-9.** *For other cases see earlier editions of this digest and the decennial digests.*

Library references

C.J.S. Names.

⊙══ **8. Mode of conferring or acquiring.**

Library references

C.J.S. Names § 3.

⊙══ **10.—Assumed names.**

D.C.Ill. 1943. At common law and in the absence of statutory restriction an individual may lawfully change his name without resort to any legal proceeding and for all purposes the name thus assumed will constitute his legal name just as though given at birth, and the rule applies though name of one's living brother or other person be assumed.

In re Leibowitz, 49 F.Supp. 953.

An alien after gaining admittance to United States under name used by him in Russia, although not the name given to him at birth, had right to assume his real name.

In re Leibowitz, 49 F.Supp. 953.

Ill. 1951. Holders of notes made payable to a fictitious named finance company under which holders were conducting their business, were not barred from obtaining judgment on notes against guarantor thereof, because they had failed to register their assumed business name with county clerk as required by statute, since penalty expressed in such fictitious name statute was exclusive. S.H.A. ch. 96, §§ 4-8.

Cohen v. Lerman, 96 N.E.2d 528, 408 Ill. 155.

Ill. 1951. Contract made by plaintiff with defendant to install furnace in defendant's residence was not rendered unenforceable because plaintiff had not registered assumed name under which he was doing business with county clerk as required by statute. S.H.A. ch. 96, § 8; ch. 114½, § 2b.

Grody v. Scalone, 96 N.E.2d 97, 408 Ill. 61.

Ill.App. 1979. Under statute requiring a certificate to register the ownership of a business operated under assumed business name, whether certain conduct occurred is a question of fact, but whether certain conduct violates the statute is a question of law to be decided by the court. S.H.A. ch. 96, § 4.

People v. Wallace, 33 Ill.Dec. 687, 397 N.E.2d 20, 77 Ill.App.3d 979.

In prosecution for transacting business without having on file a required certificate to register the ownership of a business operated under an assumed business name, the trial court did not err in making determination that the complaint failed to state cause of action prior to trial on ground that statute required questions of fact to be decided by jury and that trial court may take factual questions from jury only at close of State's evidence, since the question whether placing of an advertisement constituted a transaction of business was a question of law rather than a question of fact, and statute does not deal with a motion to dismiss a criminal complaint for failure to state an offense. S.H.A. ch. 38, §§ 114-2, 115-4(a, k).

People v. Wallace, 33 Ill.Dec. 687, 397 N.E.2d 20, 77 Ill.App.3d 979.

The purpose of statute regulating the conducting of business under an assumed name is to provide the public with access to information concerning the identity of those conducting businesses under names other than their own, and to protect individuals who might deal with or give credit to a fictitious entity. S.H.A. ch. 96, § 4.

People v. Wallace, 33 Ill.Dec. 687, 397 N.E.2d 20, 77 Ill.App.3d 979.

The defendants' placing of advertisement in newspaper soliciting orders for pregnancy test kit accompanied by guaranteed payment constituted the "transaction of business" within statute making it unlawful to conduct business under an assumed name without having filed with clerk of county a certificate advising that such business would be conducted under an assumed name. S.H.A. ch. 96, § 4.

People v. Wallace, 33 Ill.Dec. 687, 397 N.E.2d 20, 77 Ill.App.3d 979.

The statute making it unlawful to conduct a business under an assumed name without having filed with clerk of county a certificate advising that such business would be conducted under an assumed name is not unconstitutionally vague as applied to defendants who were charged with "knowingly" violating the statute, since "knowingly" implies that the act was "performed consciously and intelligently, with actual knowledge of the facts and the law's requirements." S.H.A. ch. 96, § 4.

People v. Wallace, 33 Ill.Dec. 687, 397 N.E.2d 20, 77 Ill.App.3d 979.

Ill.App. 1972. Statute making it unlawful to conduct a business under an assumed name without having filed with clerk of county a certificate advising that such business would be conducted under an assumed name and without complying with publication requirements for such a business does not impose absolute liability for its violation; there must be intent to contravene its terms. S.H.A. ch. 38, §§ 1-1 et seq., 4-3(a), 4-4 to 4-7, 4-9; ch. 96, §§ 4, 4 to 8a, 8.

People v. Arnold, 279 N.E.2d 436, 3 Ill. App.3d 678.

Ill.App. 1960. In suit to recover on oral contract for plaintiff's revision and installation

For legislative history of cited statutes

None of these is better than the others. Whichever one your library has is fine.

My local library has Illinois Decisions. The citation is to 33 Ill. Dec. 687, so I looked up the case by using the first number—33—to know to go to the volume of Illinois Decisions, numbered 33, and the second number—687—to know to turn to page 687. See how easy it is? And shown on page 34 is a copy of the case, *People v. Wallace*, which I found there. This is a case just like the hundreds of cases every student reads in law school. With a little practice you can be a fluent reader of cases, too. See the headnotes? Everything before Kasserman, Justice, is not part of the official decision. These are like little study aids to help you understand the facts and issues and ruling in the case. In this case, headnote 4 references the purpose of the assumed name statute. If that was the only part of the case you were interested in, you could go directly to paragraph 4,5 on page 690 and read just that section of the decision.

Yes, I understand that I make it sound easy and that using a law library for the first time can be intimidating. Ask the librarian to help you if you get stuck. If you really can't find an answer or if you find an answer but you don't understand it, don't fret; there are other resources available. In fact, see the chapter An Embarrassment of Resources.

Law Outside the Law Library

Sometimes by looking up the law you will be reinventing the wheel. For example, you might not want to read every statute or case about how to get a trademark when there are dozens of books on that very subject outside of the law library. In your public library you will find self-help law books in the 340 section of the stacks, assuming your library uses the Dewey Decimal system.

PEOPLE v. WALLACE

by complaint to the Illinois Industrial Commission pursuant to section 19(k) of the Workmen's Compensation Act (Ill.Rev.Stat.1977, ch. 48, par. 138.19(k)) which section provides for the allowance of 50% additional compensation of the amount payable at the time of the award.

For the reasons stated, the judgment of the circuit court of St. Clair County is affirmed.

AFFIRMED.

JONES, P. J., and KARNS, J., concur.

---

77 Ill.App.3d 979
397 N.E.2d 20

**PEOPLE of the State of Illinois,
Plaintiff-Appellant,**

v.

**Charlene and Kennis WALLACE,
Defendants-Appellees.**

No. 78-380.

**Appellate Court of Illinois,
Fifth District.**

Oct. 15, 1979.

The State appealed from an order of the Circuit Court, Saline County, Arlie O. Boswell, J., which granted defendants' motion to dismiss a criminal complaint for failure to state a cause of action. The Appellate Court, Kasserman, J., held that: (1) whether certain conduct occurred is a question of fact, but whether certain conduct violates a certain statute is a question of law to be decided by the court; (2) evidence presented at trial need not be limited to transaction set out in bill of particulars; (3) the purpose of the statute regulating conducting of business under assumed name is to provide public with access to information concerning identity of those conducting businesses under names other than their own, and to protect individuals who might deal with or give credit to a fic-

titious entity; (4) defendants' solicitation of orders accompanied by guaranteed payment constituted the "transaction of business" within the statute; and (5) the statute is not unconstitutionally vague.

Reversed and remanded.

1. Names ⊱⟞ 10

Under statute requiring a certificate to register the ownership of a business operated under assumed business name, whether certain conduct occurred is a question of fact, but whether certain conduct violates the statute is a question of law to be decided by the court. S.H.A. ch. 96, § 4.

2. Indictment and Information ⊱⟞ 121.5

In prosecution for transacting business without having on file required certificate to register ownership of a business operated under an assumed business name, it was proper for trial court to consider whether the transaction stated in State's bill of particulars constituted an offense despite contention that bill of particulars should not limit State's proof on the trial and that, as a consequence, the trial court prematurely made determination that the charge did not state an offense. S.H.A. ch. 38, §§ 3-3(b), 114-2; ch. 96, § 4.

3. Names ⊱⟞ 10

In prosecution for transacting business without having on file a required certificate to register the ownership of a business operated under an assumed business name, the trial court did not err in making determination that the complaint failed to state cause of action prior to trial on ground that statute required questions of fact to be decided by jury and that trial court may take factual questions from jury only at close of State's evidence, since the question whether placing of an advertisement constituted a transaction of business was a question of law rather than a question of fact, and statute does not deal with a motion to dismiss a criminal complaint for failure to state an offense. S.H.A. ch. 38, §§ 114-2, 115-4(a, k).

People v. Wallace

4. Names ⟪⟫ **10**

The purpose of statute regulating the conducting of business under an assumed name is to provide the public with access to information concerning the identity of those conducting businesses under names other than their own, and to protect individuals who might deal with or give credit to a fictitious entity. S.H.A. ch. 96, § 4.

5. Names ⟪⟫ **10**

The defendants' placing of advertisement in newspaper soliciting orders for pregnancy test kit accompanied by guaranteed payment constituted the "transaction of business" within statute making it unlawful to conduct business under an assumed name without having filed with clerk of county a certificate advising that such business would be conducted under an assumed name. S.H.A. ch. 96, § 4.

See publication Words and Phrases for other judicial constructions and definitions.

6. Names ⟪⟫ **10**

The statute making it unlawful to conduct a business under an assumed name without having filed with clerk of county a certificate advising that such business would be conducted under an assumed name is not unconstitutionally vague as applied to defendants who were charged with "knowingly" violating the statute, since "knowingly" implies that the act was "performed consciously and intelligently, with actual knowledge of the facts and the law's requirements." S.H.A. ch. 96, § 4.

See publication Words and Phrases for other judicial constructions and definitions.

Walden E. Morris, State's Atty., Harrisburg, Raymond F. Buckley, Jr., Deputy Director, Ann E. Singleton, Staff Atty., State's Attys. Appellate Service Commission, Mount Vernon, for plaintiff-appellant.

Robert H. Rath, Harrisburg, for defendants-appellees.

KASSERMAN, Justice:

This is an appeal by the State from an order granting defendant's motion to dismiss a criminal complaint for failure to state a cause of action.

The defendants were charged by criminal complaint with violating Ill.Rev.Stat.1977, ch. 96, par. 4 by transacting business as Quickway Enterprises without having on file with the County Clerk of Saline County the required certificate to register the ownership of a business operated under an assumed business name. The defendants, without counsel, pleaded guilty to the charge and were fined. Subsequently, the defendants obtained counsel, who filed motions in arrest of judgment. These motions were granted because the original complaints did not allege that the defendants acted with the requisite mental state, i. e., "knowingly."

The same day, the State filed seven criminal complaints charging that the defendants had knowingly transacted business as Quickway Enterprises in violation of Ill.Rev.Stat.1977, ch. 96, par. 4 on October 13 through October 19, 1976. The defendants filed a motion for discovery and a motion for a bill of particulars, which were duly answered by the State. In its answer to the motion for a bill of particulars, the State asserted that the defendants violated the statute by transacting business through advertisement to the public in the Daily Egyptian Newspaper, Southern Illinois University, Carbondale, Illinois, and by promoting the sale of a product by public advertisement through the circulation area of the Daily Egyptian Newspaper. Attached to the State's answer to the bill of particulars was a reproduced copy of the Daily Egyptian Newspaper of October 13, 1976, which contained the following advertisement:

PREGNANCY TEST. RUN your own pregnancy test in the privacy of your home with our complete pregnancy test kit, including all test material and easy to follow directions. This simple urine test gives accurate results within two minutes. Send $12.50 money order for each test to: Quickway Enterprises, Box 42, Carrier Mills, IL 62917

The defendants filed motions to dismiss the complaints alleging four grounds for dismissal. Three of these grounds, that prosecution was barred by Section 3-3(b) of the Criminal Code, that prosecution was barred by the due process clauses of the Illinois and Federal Constitutions, and that the Statute was unconstitutionally vague, were rejected by the trial court. The fourth ground, that the charges do not state offenses, was the basis of the trial court's order dismissing the complaints. Specifically, the trial court stated:

"I believe that mere solicitation is not what is meant by the transaction of business unless it happens to be the business to solicit. I think that it would not have been enough under the civil rules for long arm, as you point out, for long arm purposes under the civil rules and I think that for it to be a crime it must be considerably more severe than in civil litigation for minimum contact satisfaction. There are multitudes of cases. Almost every state has a case dealing with doing business, giving courts jurisdiction, under long arm statutes, and the corporation trust company has a whole volume dealing with the question of doing business. I don't think that mere solicitation unaccompanied by sales or other activities particularly, if it's merely—I get the feeling from what's been said here, maybe this is incorrect, but at least I got the feeling that there was a single ad placed and multiple runnings of the ad. I don't know whether that is true or not. At least that's what I gathered from what Mr. Rath stated. If that's so, it would be a single act of placing the ad—if it's transacting business at all it would be that single act, not the multiple running that I think is involved. But here again, to invite one to do business isn't necessarily the transacting of business, and I think from what I have heard here, that the implication is that the business that they were really going to be engaged in was that of selling products and in the absence of a transac-

tion with somebody who was a prospective purchaser and I have this doubt that you have shown a transaction of business that is prohibited by the statute."

The State made no effort to amend either the charges or the bill. The trial court granted defendant's motion to dismiss, and this appeal by the State followed.

[1] The State first contends that the trial court erred in deciding an issue of fact prior to trial. This portion of the State's argument is based upon the proposition that whether the advertisement in the newspaper constituted transacting business under the statute in question was a question of fact for the jury. We disagree. Whether certain conduct occurred is a question of fact, but whether certain conduct violates a certain statute is a question of law to be decided by the court. The portion of the State's argument which is predicated upon this issue being one of fact rather than one of law must, therefore, be rejected.

[2] The defendants first contend that after the State had answered the bill of particulars, any evidence it presents at trial must be limited to the transactions set out in the bill of particulars.

The Illinois Supreme Court, in *People v. Bain* (1935) 359 Ill. 455, 195 N.E. 42, stated:

"The object of a bill of particulars is to give the defendant notice of the specific charges against him and to inform him of the particular transactions in question, so that he may be prepared to make his defense. (Citations). Its effect, therefore, is to limit the evidence to the transactions set out in the bill of particulars. The prosecution, however, is not required to specify in the bill all the evidence it will produce in support of the charges. The object of such a bill is not to make a substantive charge against the defendant but to restrict the evidence which may be introduced under the indictment to the particular transactions." (People v. Bain (1935) 359 Ill. 455, 472, 195 N.E. 42, 50.)

The State contends that the bill of particulars should not limit its proof on the trial and that, as a consequence, the trial court prematurely made the determination that the charge did not state an offense. We do not agree. If the State's contention were followed, proof of acts of the defendants other than the placing of the advertisement but constituting the "transaction of business" should be permitted at trial. Such is not the design of Section 114-2 of the Code of Criminal Procedure of 1963 (Ill.Rev.Stat.1977, ch. 38, par. 114-2), covering motions for bills of particulars. This statute requires that they "shall specify the particulars of the offense necessary to enable the defendant to prepare his defense." To permit the State to introduce evidence at trial of acts of the defendants other than the placing of the advertisements would be to permit the State to subject defendants to the element of surprise, a result certainly not contemplated by Section 114-2 of the Code of Criminal Procedure and a result which we will not condone. Therefore, under Bain, it was proper for the trial court to consider whether the transactions stated in the bill of particulars constituted an offense.

[3] The State also argues that Section 115-4(a) of the Code of Criminal Procedures of 1963 (Ill.Rev.Stat.1977, ch. 38, par. 115-4(a)), requires that questions of fact shall be decided by the jury and that the trial court may take factual questions from the jury only at the close of the State's evidence. The State's reliance upon Section 115-4(a) is misplaced for two reasons. First, as discussed above, the question of whether or not the placing of an advertisement constituted the transaction of business is a question of law rather than a question of fact. Second, Section 115-4(k), and not Section 115-4(a), deals with a directed verdict of not guilty, with a judgment of acquittal and discharge of the defendant at the close of the State's evidence or at the close of all the evidence. In this case a motion to dismiss a criminal complaint for failure to state an offense was involved. No jeopardy attached, and had the State chosen to file amended complaints, it could have done so. Therefore, the trial court did not err in making the determination prior to trial.

Next, the State questions the correctness of the court's determination that the placing of the advertisement did not constitute the transaction of business under Ill.Rev.Stat.1977, ch. 96, par. 4. This statute provides that "No person or persons shall conduct or transact business in this State under an assumed name * * *" without filing a specified certificate in the office of the county clerk of the county "* * * in which such person or persons conduct or transact or intend to conduct or transact such business * * *." The statute does not define what constitutes the conduct or transaction of business.

We are not aware of any case interpreting the phrase "* * * conduct or transact business * * *" within the meaning of the statute concerning assumed business names. The trial court, as stated earlier, concluded that mere solicitation of business was not conducting or transacting business, in the absence of a sale. The trial court considered cases interpreting transaction of business within the meaning of establishing the due process minimum contact to establish civil "long arm" jurisdiction over nonresidents under the applicable statute (Ill.Rev.Stat.1977, ch. 110, par. 17(1)). The State argues that the trial court erred in considering the civil "long arm" cases in its determination of this case. Furthermore, the State contends that the trial court erred in indicating that the definition of "transacting business" should involve a higher level of activity for criminal prosecutions than for establishing *in personam* jurisdiction in civil cases. It should be noted, however, that the trial court stated that it did not feel that these cases were controlling and expressly distinguished them from this criminal case.

[4, 5] The purpose of the act regulating the conducting of business under an assumed name is to provide the public with access to information concerning the identity of those conducting businesses under names other than their own, and to protect individuals who might deal with or give credit to a fictitious entity. (*People v. Arnold* (1st Dist. 1972) 3 Ill.App.3d 678,

279 N.E.2d 436; cf. *Curtis v. Albion-Brown's Post 590* (5th Dist. 1966) 74 Ill.App.2d 144, 219 N.E.2d 386.) In this case the activity which the State contends constituted the transaction of business was the placing of a newspaper advertisement. In spite of the fact that the State did not allege that the defendants sold, or contracted to sell, any products nor that they sought or extended credit or dealt directly with any potential customer, the abuses sought to be curbed by the statute may well have arisen from their placing of the advertisement. The advertisement solicited the general public to "Send $12.50 money order for each test to: Quickway Enterprises, Box 42, Carrier Mills, IL 62917." The proof on trial quite possibly may have established that several payments were in fact made to defendants and no test kits furnished by them. In our opinion, such evidence would constitute ample proof of a violation of the statute under the charges and under the bill of particulars. If the purpose of the statute governing the registration of assumed business names is to provide the public with the identity of the fictitious entity with whom the public might deal or give credit to, as stated in *Arnold*, we can conceive of no greater need for such protection than from a business entity soliciting prepaid orders under an artificial name such as used by the defendants. Therefore, we conclude that the defendants' solicitation, or invitation, of orders accompanied by guaranteed payments constituted the transaction of business under Ill.Rev.Stat.1977, ch. 96, par. 4.

[6] Defendants finally contend that since the statute in question does not state when the required certificate must be filed, it is unconstitutionally vague. The statute requires that the specified certificate be filed in the office of the County Clerk of the County "* * * in which such person or persons conduct or transact or intend to conduct or transact such business * *." (Ill.Rev.Stat.1977, ch. 96, par. 4.) It clearly contemplates the possibility of filing before transacting any business and expressly permits filing during or after transacting business. Defendants argue that because of this alleged defect, the statute in question is unconstitutionally vague. It is contended that defendants may now file the required certificate and not be in violation of the statute since it sets no time limit on the filing. We do not agree.

Defendants were charged with "knowingly" violating the statute in the amended complaints. The court in *Arnold* established the necessity of charging that defendants knowingly violated the statute governing the registration of assumed business names. It was there stated that "knowingly" implies that the act was "performed consciously and intelligently, with actual knowledge of the facts and the law's requirements." (*People v. Arnold*, 3 Ill.App.3d 678, 682, 279 N.E.2d 436, 439.) Defendants are here charged with knowledge of the requirement to register and with knowingly violating the act. This obviously satisfies defendants' contention that "any prosecution under this statute which does not require that they [defendants] knew or should have known of the requirement to register with the County Clerk would violate the due process clauses of the Illinois and Federal Constitutions."

For the foregoing reasons, the judgment of the circuit court of Saline County is reversed and this cause is remanded to the circuit court of Saline County for further proceedings not inconsistent with this opinion.

REVERSED and REMANDED.

JONES, P. J., and HARRISON, J., concur.

You'll find books on how to get a trademark or copyright; how to write a will; how to draw up a simple contract; in fact, how to do just about any legal thing you'd want to do. You will even find books there that will help you do legal research.

Believe it or not, I don't know everything. When I do, you will see me on *Jeopardy*. So when I need to know about an area of the law that is completely new to me, I sometimes use books intended for non-lawyers. They often give a good overview of a subject.

For example, I decided recently that I wanted a trademark for a name I want to use for my business. I wasn't too sure if I could apply by myself or if I needed a special lawyer, so I got a book from the library called *Trademark: Legal Care for Your Business & Product Name*, which is published by the well-known do-it-yourself law guide publisher, Nolo Press. The book doesn't have page numbers, so I can't tell you how many pages it is, but it's the size of a small phone book. Frankly, it told me much more than I'll ever want or need to know about trademarks. I really just wanted the form and instructions on how to fill out the form. The book gave me that, as well as a phone number to call for the federal trademark office's information help line. (This number is also printed right on the trademark application form.)

If you get the form or the number (703-308-HELP), you can call and get an instruction book for free. The free book is simple, and easy to understand. Nolo also has a similar book on copyrights, but again, if you get the form and the instructions, you probably don't need a book. Ask your librarian for help in finding the form and the instructions, or find the information on the Internet. Practically every government office or agency has a web site.

Lawyers have access to legal databases like Lexis and Westlaw, which you may have heard about, but these are very expensive. Within limits, you can also do some legal research on-line. If you have a case name and citation and the case is not too old, you can probably find it on-line. On the other hand, if you need an overview of the law, you will probably need to start your search in a law library. For on-line research, the best site I have found is www.Legalonline.com. It contains a sort of index to all the other on-line legal research sites, for statutes and for cases, so it is a great place to start.

Nolo Press also puts out a resource (book and disk), called *Legal Research On-line and in the Library*, which may be of some help, but I found it hard to use. In fact, I installed the disk on my drive, couldn't figure out how to use it, and then crashed some of my other software after I uninstalled it. I say, start at the library. Get comfortable there. Then familiarize yourself with the on-line sites if you have Internet access. No need to spend money on books or disks. Just do it.

3

Win the Battle *and* the War

(THE ART OF NEGOTIATION)

All of life is a negotiation. We are not born with negotiation skills, just as we are not born with table manners. However, we start to figure out negotiating tactics from the moment we are born. Think of negotiating principles as the table manners of life. The first example of both is this not-too-elaborate deal: Bring me milk and I will stop screaming my wee head off. Sounds like a reasonable—and effective—bargaining position! The resulting transaction provides the most basic of eating etiquette and negotiation skills. Parents learn from this exchange, too. They try bargaining for a few extra minutes of sleep. Sometimes this works, and more often it doesn't.

Relationships are a series of negotiations. We negotiate with our coworkers and bosses, with our loved ones and friends, and with service and sales people. The nature of the relationship determines the basis of the negotiation.

Children's negotiations are akin to bribery. Mom says, "Let the nice doctor look in your ear now, and I will buy you an ice cream cone on the way home." Or Tommy says to Dad, "*Pleeeeease* let me sleep over at Charlie's and I'll keep my room clean for a whole month." Children come to understand and play this process with their parents adeptly. A mom who can make a dozen subordinates at work stay late to finish a project sometimes has difficulty negotiating whether Sally will eat just three more bites of her dinner, or whether Sally will eat no more at all.

Childhood negotiation skills become the building blocks for all of our adult relationships, but very often the rules change, just as our relationships change. The relationship between a husband and wife is different from any other relationship, literally. No two marriages are the same in the way that the couple negotiates their roles in general, or as it relates to the little stuff, day to day. Similarly, what works in negotiations with your husband will not always work in negotiations with your boss, coworker, or subordinate in the office. And a whole other kind of negotiation is needed to deal with the painting contractor, flea market salesman, or long-distance telephone service provider.

As a lawyer, I've developed effective negotiating skills for a variety of situations. In fact, one of the best ways to "win" a lawsuit for a client is not in the courtroom, but at the negotiation table. So I've laid out the basic principles that I use all the time and that you can successfully apply to your own life.

Margaret's Tricks of the Negotiation Trade

#1: Get Smart

So, how do you get the best deal and "kill" your co-negotiator? Go into the negotiation smart. If you are buying a new water heater for the first time ever from someone who sells water heaters for a living, *do your research*. Go to the library. Check out the *Consumer Reports* issue on water heaters. Read articles on water heater fraud. Research water heaters on the Internet. If you don't have a computer, your local library will give you access to the World Wide Web and even show you how to find water heater Internet sites. Find out if you really need a new water heater, or if your existing water heater can be repaired. Know which size would be best for you before you go to buy one or you will be sold the most expensive one the salesman can negotiate. Also, understand the other features of water heaters, like energy efficiency, so you can compare.

Remember that most salespeople work on commission, so they want to make the most profitable sale *for them*. Even if yours is not on commission, he wants to make a good sale. That is how he justifies his existence to his employer. It's really not his problem if he sells you a water heater that's too big or too small for your needs. It *will* become your problem if you buy the wrong one. And it is always better—and cheaper—to avoid a problem in the first place than to fix one later.

Once you know what kind of water heater you need for your home you can start comparing water heater dealers. Does the price include installation? Will they take away your old water heater? Ask your neighbors where they bought their water heaters and what kind of experience they had. Were they happy with their choice? Did they get what they were promised? How was the service? Referrals like this are often the best way to get reliable information.

Never forget that almost *every* aspect of an exchange is negotiable, from price to service. If the salesman can't alter the price, can he throw in the removal of the old water heater (or sofa or sink)? Ask if a cash deal can be done more cheaply than a credit card transaction. And if your homework included getting written estimates or "bids" on a job, and it should, you can say, "Joe's gives installation free. What can you do for me?" Jack might say, well, then go to Joe's. On the other hand, Jack might throw in free installation and agree to get rid of your old heater, too. If you don't ask, you don't get.

Of course, it is easier to negotiate for an item that is widely available from a number of sources. If you want a 20-cubic-foot refrigerator with ice and water dispensers, and every department and appliance store in town sells a model that meets your criteria, then you can simply call around for the best deal—including price and service (delivery of the new one and removal of the old). If, on the other hand, you need a weird-sized sleeve air conditioner for a thirty-year-old condo and only one place in town carries it, you will pay their asking price or you will sweat out the summer. This is simple supply and demand. It's like comparing a Tickle Me Elmo to Legos. It is the reason some things are negotiable and others not.

#2: Know When to Go In for the Kill

Once you are armed with information, you can go for the throat in certain negotiations. Some things in life are negotiable and some are not. "I don't care to pay six thousand dollars in taxes this year. I will give you three" is not just laughable, it is criminal. Luckily, however, there are times when you *can* stand firm, when you have nothing or not too much to lose by holding steady on a position. This is generally when you are buying something that you want but don't need, and is readily available in some quantity. Negotiations of this kind can be the most fun or the most trying, depending on your perspective. But keep in mind that while you're going in for the kill, your "opposition" will be doing the same.

The best example of this kind of negotiation is the kind we all look forward to excitedly—the new car transaction. I know we all wish we could negotiate with those pleasant salesmen more often just to try to get the better of them, but alas, for most of us, this process takes place only every few years. The car salesman, on the other hand, negotiates similar transactions *for a living*.

Please don't think I am picking on car salesmen. As a lawyer I can ill afford to stereotype any group of people, and lawyers and car salesmen are the butt of more jokes than all other professions lumped together. So you may substitute any other salesperson into these scenarios—the water heater salesman, the carpet salesman. The point is, you're negotiating with a professional dealmaker. It's not necessary to feel any compassion for this person. Don't worry that his twelve children will have no socks to wear this winter if you don't pay that extra five hundred dollars for your dream car. Get the best deal you can get. The salesman will *not* be losing money on the deal, I guarantee it. If you pay five hundred dollars less for the car than the patsy before you paid for the same vehicle, this is a *good* thing. It's not something which should cause you any discomfort or regret. You should throw a party with the money you saved (and invite me). You should toast your good fortune at having such a lovely new car and such smart negotiating skills. You should not invite the salesman, as that would defeat the Never See This Person Again premise.

Unlike a family member or boss or next-door neighbor, the salesman will not be in a position to punish you for negotiating too well. Nor will his feelings be hurt when you win. This is exactly the point. There are two kinds of negotiations. One is a one-time transaction—in our example, a car sale. In other negotiations, like with your employer or employee, ramifications of the negotiation can affect you adversely after it's over—you have to maintain a relationship with the person. But you don't have to maintain a relationship with the car dealer unless you really want to. Car, home, and appliance sales fall into this category. Of course, the other party can also pick up the marbles by refusing to sell—or buy—at your price. That is okay. No hard feelings. There are other cars, houses, and appliances for sale. This is the essence of this game. Each party to the transaction looks out for *her* best interests.

I had a judge once tell me that he feels a negotiation is successful if neither party feels satisfied with the result. I think that notion is a bunch of hooey. If I'm not happy with a deal, I don't do it. A good deal is one about which both parties feel good, but in the one-battle war you only have to worry about your own needs. You don't have to wake up with your car salesman in the morning or see his face across the break room at work. The deal is the deal and then you each get on with your lives.

My experience is that many women have difficulty with the concept of worrying only about their own feelings. Some women want to nurture and care for everyone, including the car salesman. They worry whether the car salesman will make his quota. If this is you, get over it. Go into the negotiation with your homework and a good idea of what you want—and that's all. Then you can be quite candid and unemotional about what you want and what you're willing to pay for it. Simple!

#3: Have a Fall Guy

It is so much easier to go for the kill if you are not the actual spear thrower. Trust me on this. You can buy a car or anything else by yourself, but it helps to have someone along who can play the fall guy. Fall guys are a tradition in male-dominated professions. Men have learned to invent fall guys. They're "silent partners" who can offer you a fault-free, guilt-exempt "out" if things don't go your way in a negotiation. I know in Chapter One I advised you not to blame others for your problems, but this is one case where you can.

As a lawyer I always have a built-in fall guy—my client. I can say, "Hey, Suzy, if it were up to me, I would do the deal on your terms, but my client says no way. Sorry. What can I tell you!" Similarly, I am the fall guy for my client. Clients can always say, "My lawyer told me not to do that. What can I tell you!" It eliminates any personal friction from a deal. For example, your boss may answer your request for a raise with something like, "You certainly deserve a raise, Jane, but I don't think the president will go for it. We're in a salary-freeze mode right now. But let me ask. I'll let you know what he says." That way, even if the deal doesn't get done (and sometimes it won't) you don't have a grudge against your boss. He went to bat for you, so it's not his fault. It's his boss's.

A fall guy is especially effective when you're buying something. Think about my car-buying example. When did you ever buy a car when the salesman didn't have his own fall guy? Never. His fall guy is called the sales manager. I guarantee you had the following conversation last time you went to buy a car:

YOU: Yes, yes, it's a lovely car.

SALESMAN: And fuchsia is *the* hot color this year.

YOU: Yes, I'm sure, but I think *forty thousand dollars* is just too much for a Dzitshu Teenyweenymobile.

SALESMAN: We are having a promotion right now and I'm entered into a contest to get a trip to Hawaii. I really want to sell you this car. What can you offer to close this deal so you can drive it off the lot today?

YOU: I think thirty-two thousand is a fair price.

SALESMAN: Oh, come on, work with me on this. You know I can't *give* you the car!

YOU: Okay. Thirty-three thousand.

SALESMAN: Well, I know he will laugh me out of his office, but I will take your offer to my sales manager.

The sales manager is the fall guy. The salesman will come back from either talking to his sales manager or having a cup of coffee and tell you, "Look, I like you. If it were up to me, I would sell you the car for the thirty-three thousand you have offered, but my sales manager says the demand for fuchsia Teenyweenymobiles is so great that they're on back order. If you want this car, you will have to come up with thirty-seven thousand dollars."

If you really want the car, you will now start to squirm. You had decided from your research that you only wanted to pay thirty-five thousand, but what if he's right? What if you don't pay the thirty-seven and they don't do the deal? Do you want to start over somewhere else? What if there is no fuchsia Teenyweenymobile anywhere else to be found? And if thirty-five thousand really is your rock bottom offer, should you offer it, or should you offer thirty-four and see if they budge?

If you had a fall guy, you wouldn't be worrying about this. The fall guy will have no interest in your car but will simply be doing or not doing your deal according to your already provided instructions. You and the fall guy will not alter your course. You will stick with the plan. This is how a car purchase should work.

My sister had her heart set on a certain model 1981 sports car, a classic two-seater with some power under the hood and some charm on the highway—a cutie car. She did her research. She knew how much this car should cost and she knew which features she had to have and which were expendable. Then she found her dream car. It was on one of the many local used car lots. I went with her to check it out. We took it for a spin (without the salesman, so we could talk). The car drove like a dream. The body was in perfect shape. We parked and checked the car out. We got down on the ground and looked under the car, although I still don't know what we were looking for. We agreed on the maximum price my sister was willing to pay for the car, and that we wanted some minimum warranty so that she could get the car checked out and, if there were some major problem, she could get the car repaired at the dealer's expense.

Then we went back to the dealer. Per our agreement with each other, my sister did not speak to the salesman. Not one word. She just smiled and deferred to me. Now remember, I was not in love with this car. I wanted my sister to have it because she apparently *was* in love with it, and I love my sister. I wanted her to have it, but I wanted her to have it on *our* terms. So began the negotiation. The dealer told me the asking price and I offered several thousand dollars less (and substantially less than my sister was willing to pay for the car). The salesman and I (with intermittent interruptions for discussions with the "sales manager") volleyed prices back and forth until the salesman was two hundred dollars from the price my sister had said she was willing to pay. So I made her final offer. After spending a morning negotiating, I finally said she was willing to pay $X. The salesman said, "I'm sorry, I just can't come down that extra two hundred dollars."

I stood up. I shook the salesman's hand. I said it was a pleasure meeting him and I was sorry we weren't going to be doing business together. I told him I was sure he would have no problem getting his price from someone else, and then I turned to leave. My poor sister got puppy dog eyes. She could *not* believe I would walk away from her beloved car just because the salesman would not meet her price. I motioned my sister to the door, and reluctantly, mournfully, she stood up. She took only one step toward the door, and the salesman said, "Oh, all right. They will laugh me out of the sales meeting, but I really want to do this deal with you, so you can have the car for your price."

My sister got the car and she got it at her price. If she had done the negotiation herself, I am sure she would have paid the extra two hundred dollars. If I had been negotiating that same deal for my own car, I probably would have paid the extra two hundred dollars, too. The key is that the person who is doing the negotiating has no emotional involvement with the deal. I can much more easily go for the kill on someone else's deal—or kill the deal—than I can negotiate on my own behalf. This is just a fact of life. Men seem to have passed this "fall guy" trick on to each other. Women should use it effectively, too.

No matter how experienced a negotiator you are, you can benefit from the fall guy trick. It's the reason lawyers, agents, and brokers EXIST. It's just plain easier for a negotiator to say, "You're lucky to have my client" than it is to say "You're lucky to have ME!"

#4: Never Negotiate Against Yourself

Think of a negotiation as a tango. It takes two. You could dance around a partner who's standing still and *call* it a tango, but you won't win the dance contest. You can try negotiating alone but you will have no bargain. It seems obvious, but I see people do it all the time. Let me illustrate with an example from a flea market:

ME: How much is this unique pre-Columbian knickknack?
FLEA-MARKET VENDOR (FMV for short): Twelve bucks.
ME: Oh, that's too much.
FMV: Oh, okay, how about ten?
ME: No, still too much.
FMV: Will you pay seven?

The flea market vendor is negotiating against himself. If you can get away with it, you can stand still and let the vendor dance around you. Eventually he will give you his best price. Do not be the one doing the dancing if your partner is standing still. It's not productive. You will not know where your co-negotiator is coming from, *and* you will be doing all the giving. Every time you move from your previous position, you have conceded and you have received nothing.

In the car negotiation that I illustrated earlier, the customer negotiated against herself. She offered thirty-two thousand dollars for a car, and when the salesman said, "Work with me on this. I can't *give* you the car," the customer said, "Oh, okay, thirty-three." Bad move from the customer's bargaining perspective. It's great if you are the salesman and you can get away with it.

Why is it so important not to negotiate against yourself? In any negotiation the party who moves the least wins. This is a basic truth of negotiation. You want your opponent to come to you, whether it's one of those go-for-the-throat, fight-to-the-death, once-in-a-lifetime transactions, or the deal with your kid over whether she will go to bed now or in an hour. If it's a car deal, you want to pay the price you came prepared to pay. If your daughter is going to be crabby and groggy all day tomorrow and you're going to suffer for it, you want her in bed now. Obviously we can't always have exactly what we want, but with effective negotiation we can get as close as possible to our goals.

Let's say you are trying to avoid filing a lawsuit, but your neighbor's dog chewed up your leg pretty badly. You've finished your extensive physical therapy and plastic surgery and you're ready to negotiate a settlement with your neighbor's home owner's insurance company. You've educated yourself as best you can, at the library and by talking to colleagues and maybe a lawyer. You've put together an impressive packet, with all of your medical bills and lost wage statements. You have before and after pictures of your leg. You sent them to the insurance adjuster, along with a letter telling her you will call to discuss settlement, and then you call. The ball is in your court. You make a demand. Let's say your educated demand, based on your research, is one hundred thousand dollars.

Ta-da. The ball is now in the insurance adjuster's court. She can volley the ball back, by accepting your demand or by making a counter offer. Simply saying, "No. Can't do that," is a fault, to borrow a tennis term. "No" does not put the ball back in your court unless you jump over the net and pick it up, which you shouldn't do. The adjuster, in order to be playing this game with you, has to expend some energy and move from her spot. If, in fact, it is her intention to offer nothing, then she should say so, and you should sue her insured—your neighbor.

If she intends to pay you something, but not what you have demanded, she should express a value. "I can't do a hundred thousand dollars, but I can do eighty" is an appropriate response. Even "No, I can't do that, but I can do twenty" is an appropriate response. Then you can judge whether to continue the negotiation or whether you are just too far apart and you need to file your lawsuit. If the adjuster says, "No, I can't do one hundred thousand, you silly fool," ignore the silly fool remark and ask, "Well, what can you do?" If you budge without a number from her, you are negotiating against yourself, which *you should never do*. Make her do the dance. Make her play the game. Do not attempt to play alone. That is Solitaire, an altogether different game. This is a *negotiation*, and it takes two.

#5: Win the Battle AND the War

I'm a much better negotiator in my professional life than I am in my personal life. I'm used to having my way. I negotiate poorly in personal relationships with people who are also used to getting their own way. "My way or the highway" is not conducive to successful personal relationships.

Women as negotiators fall into three groups. The first group is women who just want to be liked. Women in this category want everyone to like them and so they give away the store in their personal and professional lives. They are generally well-liked personally but they are professional disasters. It's hard to win Miss Congeniality and win the award for best negotiator, too. We can call this group the Kissy-Faces.

The second group are the women who like to win. They expect to be treated with respect, and in some cases, feared. They want to be taken seriously and because they think they are always right, they expect those around them to accede to their demands. They can be very successful professionally, especially if they're not *too* righteous, but their social lives are sometimes lacking. I put myself in this category. We can call these women the I'm Not Budgin' group.

The third group is the type to which we should all aspire. They know when to bark and when to bite and they know when to cuddle and make those cute little cooing noises. They can be tough, demanding businesswomen, negotiating effectively in the boardroom and across the bargaining table, but they are compassionate human beings, too.

These women have the best of both worlds. They are the Oprah Winfreys of the world. They are respected in all arenas. They have lots of genuine friends and loving families because they give so much without asking much in return. They are respected by their colleagues. They understand their different roles. They know when to go for the kill and when winning the battle will not justify losing the war. Their bosses love them because they do their homework and they bring back the spoils of war without being disagreeable. Women in this category have mastered the negotiation that is life. We can call them the Life Masters.

If you are a Life Master, congratulations. You understand what it's all about. You have achieved what all the rest of us have been seeking—or should be seeking—from life. Maybe you can take the time to mentor one of us who has not quite figured out the delicate balance that being a Life Master requires.

As an acknowledged I'm Not Budgin' woman I have a tendency to play the "my way or the highway" game (I *am* always right, after all). I'm thrilled to be respected as an attorney and agent and author. I have lots of friends, and good ones, but I know I have to learn how to budge.

Women who are Kissy-Faces know it, too. They are constantly being put upon, asked to do things that they would rather not do, but they do them so they will be liked. I have news for you Kissy-Faces. The rest of us will still like you even if you do say "no" now and then. None of us is expected to do everything for everyone *all* the time. Kissy-Faces need to learn how to say no. Next time someone makes what you feel is an unreasonable request (Why should you be the one to always have to stay and lock up? Why should the post-prom party be at your house?), just say no. People may treat you differently: They will respect you. And you will respect yourself.

When women refuse to compromise or concede any point, or conversely, when they agree to every demand and request, they automatically deny themselves opportunities to get what they want. Keep your eye on the prize, but your focus on the big picture. Negotiate life as a master.

#6: Money Isn't Everything

More money is not always better. At some point, when you have all the money you need, more will not make you happier. The unhappiest person I have ever known had a personal fortune of two hundred million dollars (give or take a million). He spent his life trying to figure out how to make more money. His personal relationships were disasters. Money is as addictive to some people as drugs or booze or the Internet are to other people. No matter how much they have, it's never enough. I think this is true for men more than for women.

Women know money is nice, but we also treasure our time and our relationships. Men are judged by how well they provide for their families, and by their toys and accoutrements. A man who does not make a lot of money is still anathema, which is sad but true.

Women should have equal pay for equal work. There is no sane argument against that, of course. But we must be ever mindful of the price of money. Men who make a lot of money very often work ridiculous hours and spend too much time away from their families. Women who make a lot of money are similarly finding that their personal relationships suffer. Sometimes time lost is the cost of money. Sometimes this can be measured in Little League games missed, or school plays unseen. Because life is a negotiation, it involves compromise. So we must make choices. Few of us could not make more money if we made different choices. We could get second (or third) jobs, but we'd be tired all the time and not much fun to be around. Some women need to work long hours to support their families and so the choice is not really a choice at all. The rest of us must decide.

The decision to further one's education is a similar compromise. Yes, it will cost a lot of money and a lot of time—years, in some cases. But maybe the sacrifice will be worth it in the long run, if it will help us get a higher rate of pay at the end, so that we will be able to work shorter hours for the same pay.

Ideally, we would all have jobs that we love, making plenty of money to pay for the lifestyles we would like to have. I'm that lucky, which is why I have been known to say that every woman should go to law school. I love arguing cases in the appellate courts, with their dark wood paneling and high ceilings and oil paintings on the walls so much that I would pay people to let me argue their cases. Lucky for me, people actually pay *me* money to do that. I am truly blessed! And I make enough money practicing law part time that I can spend time doing other things I love that don't pay as well, like writing. I could make even more money if I worked long hours, like many attorneys in big firms are forced to do—if they want to make partner—but I choose not to. Making money is not what my life is about. I work to live because I like what I do.

I negotiated the deal for this book all by myself, without a fall guy, which was stressful and may or may not have been a good tactic. Maybe I could have gotten more money from another publisher, maybe not. This book is not about money to me, though. I had the notion that I wanted to help women be empowered. I found a wonderful group of women at HarperCollins who understand my concept. They believe in me and what I am trying to do with this book. I know they will support the book when it hits the shelves and until then I have my editor standing over me, prodding me mercilessly (while I roll on the floor laughing) and holding my hand during the rough times (this is my first book, after all). So, I made a decision in the middle of the night that I could not possibly do better than to work with this group of people, for any amount of money.

When it comes to negotiations about money, the trick is that it's not all about the money. More money is not always a better deal. *Get the deal that gives you the best quality of life. If that means more money, great!*

#7: Treat People Right

Do unto others, as they say. You have only one reputation, and like it or not, you are your reputation. If you have a reputation as a crook, people will *not* do business with you and you might as well pack it up. Otherwise, make sure you deliver on your promises. If you negotiate a business deal, you must produce what you have agreed to provide. If the deal was a gross of hand-painted Santas by Sunday, you had better have them, and they had better all look like the sample. Don't make promises you can't keep.

All of us sometimes make deals we wish we hadn't once we get into them. We miscalculate the amount of time it will take to produce the product, or we didn't take into account that the costs of the raw ingredients would rise. Tough. Be a POW—Person Of Your Word. You might take a killing on one deal, but it shouldn't break you as a person. Over the course of your life you will do hundreds of deals. Live and learn from your mistakes. It's a cliché, but it's true. Here are two examples. Both involve women. I don't know why women are so poor at this game, except that men have passed the rules of business on to their sons and women have not been in business long enough to pass them on to their daughters. I learned a lot of this from my dad.

About ten years ago, I got a new job. My sister was buying a new home and I had agreed to do the closing. I did all the preliminary work on the closing but I was reluctant to take a day off from my new job to attend the closing. I hired a friend of mine from law school. She told me she would charge $150, which I thought was high, but she was my friend and so I figured she must need the money and I agreed. After the closing, she sent me a bill for $510, explaining that the closing was more work than she expected. Now, think about this. We agreed to a flat fee. We did not negotiate an hourly fee; I would not have agreed to one, at any rate. I didn't trick this woman into the original deal. She knew what she was getting into, and then she tried to renegotiate the deal after the fact. I sent her a check for the $150 we had originally agreed to, and I marked the check full payment. She wrote to my sister and pleaded for the balance of the $510, telling my sister that she and I had agreed to $150 but the closing had been more work than she expected. My sister was embarrassed and so was I. Needless to say, I have not done business with this friend again.

Another woman from my law school class was just starting her own practice about the same time that I took my new job. I agreed to send her all my criminal and divorce matters in exchange for one third of the fee. I had already done some of the work on these matters and so my one-third was justified. Sure enough, this woman, on the first matter she handled for me, was paid $2,700. I called her to see when I could expect my $900, but she hid from me for weeks. Finally she left a message on my machine at home in the middle of the day—she couldn't face me—telling me not to hold my breath, she wasn't sending a check. I did not sue this woman. I did not smear her name around town. I let it go. Nine hundred dollars lost did not break me. The loss of referrals from me may have broken her, though.

Neither of these two women was able to sustain a private practice. Both have not-very-well-regarded positions working for the state. I, on the other hand, have referred hundreds of cases since then. Only once did another lawyer try to renegotiate our deal after the fact. He told me the case had been more work than he expected and he wanted to give me less than he had originally agreed to. I said we had a deal, but that if he sent me less I guess I'd have to take it. I wasn't going to sue him for the difference or report him to the disciplinary board. I didn't even threaten to stop sending him business. He thought better of his decision anyway, and paid me the full amount he had originally agreed to. I have sent him more business since then than I have sent any other two lawyers combined. I know I can trust him to do the right thing, by me and by my clients.

Never get nasty in negotiations. This is how litigation attorneys like me cull out the pretenders. Litigators never get personal. We treat each other politely and with respect. We know our opponent's stubbornness is not a reflection on us. He is doing his job. We know that if he likes us he is more likely to go the extra mile for us. If my opposing counsel likes me (and what's not to like?), he will at least *try* to get the extra ten thousand dollars I need to make my client happy and settle a case. If I am a shrew to him, he will be happy if I am left to squirm mercilessly before my client. I hope this won't shock anyone, but the best of us duke it out in court, or across a bargaining table, and then we go for a drink. Win or lose, we are still friends. I don't mean that we have to buy Christmas presents for each others' kids, but we are always cordial. We don't hold grudges. We don't burn bridges. It's a small world (you know the song) and even within big cities there are small communities, of lawyers, doctors, florists, and booksellers, among other things. If you get a reputation for treating people right, you may lose a battle now and then, but you will definitely win the war.

#8: Strength in Numbers

We women need to stick together. We are notorious organizers and advocates. Think of Carry Nation and Susan B. Anthony. When we women take up a cause, we plot and plan and we reach our goals. That's why every good charity fundraising committee is run by women. We get the job done.

Women are a force to be reckoned with, and the more we stick together the more power we will have collectively and individually. As any Teamster can tell you, organized groups can negotiate more effectively than individuals can. This applies to people, corporations, even governments. Think about NATO and OPEC. It's hard to stare down a united front.

America's seniors are about as unified a group as you will find. Because they stick together and often vote together (or threaten to), Social Security, Medicare, and other issues of importance to aging Americans are always on the political front burner.

Women need to speak with one voice if we are to be heard and appreciated. Women have made tremendous political strides, of course. We couldn't even vote for the first half of the history of the U.S. Remember that in order for one person or group to gain power, someone else has to lose power. When women gained the right to vote, the votes of men were diluted. It was men, though, who had to agree to give women that power. Women organized and used all their energy and efforts and persuaded the men to let them vote.

Women need to organize and use all their energy to overcome workplace disparity. According to various statistics, women earn about sixty cents for every dollar a man earns. So few women make more than men do. Generally, though, jobs that are traditionally held by males pay more than jobs traditionally held by females. Truck drivers make more than child care workers. Why? Go back and ask a Teamster.

If all the lawyers in the world disappeared tomorrow, nobody would notice. If all the truck drivers disappeared, there would be no bread or milk at the markets. So, truck drivers organized and negotiated as a group, and together they had more power than they each had individually. They said, "If you want milk and bread, pay us more money." Is truck driving more demanding or higher skilled than child care? What if all the child care workers disappeared tomorrow? There'd be chaos! What if all the child care workers in the country said, "If you want safe, healthful care for your children, pay us more"? That's one heck of a bargaining position. Never forget that life is a negotiation. Women!! Together, we're a powerful group.

#9: *Quid pro Quo*

Sometimes negotiations are one-sided. Governments, teachers, and bosses make rules that are often non-negotiable. But even when we have the power to impose our will on others, it is important to treat others reasonably in negotiations. There is a doctrine called *quid pro quo*. Basically it means something for something. If you change the status quo, because you can, you should give something if you are getting something or taking something away. An employee who has been given an hour for lunch up until now is going to be none too happy to be told that from now on she gets only a half hour. The same goes for kids and curfews. If Johnny has always been told to be home by ten, he is going to be pretty mad if his curfew is changed to nine without a good reason. Part of being responsible is exercising our power reasonably. That usually means giving something for something.

Be a good and responsible negotiator. If you make a bad deal, deal with it. If you screw up, fess up. Sometimes we miscalculate. Sometimes we can't deliver. Sometimes it's our own fault, and sometimes it's not. Sometimes it's nobody's fault at all. Just don't forget your reputation.

Once, against my better judgment, I agreed to represent a major international corporation on a contingency basis in a contract dispute. In other words, I would be paid one-third of what I won for my client. It turned out that the case was not a good one. The employee of the corporation who hired me left out some important facts when I agreed to take the case. I was doing too much work on the case, and there was a chance we could lose (and I don't like to lose). It never occurred to me to change the deal, though, because I am a professional, and I stick by my terms.

One day, though, the president of this huge company called me from Germany. He had been filled in on the litigation, and he needed to talk to me, he said. His company—my client—had not been forthright with me from the beginning, he told me, and so he wanted me to settle the case and keep *all* the money, not just the one-third we had agreed to. I was pretty surprised, and the offer was tempting, but I did not accept. I told him, no, that I would settle the case, if he felt it was in the firm's best interest, but I would take only the one-third we had agreed upon; I was a professional, I told him, and I understood the risks when I agreed to represent the company on a contingent fee basis. What I was thinking was what a dope I was for making a bad deal to begin with, but that I would learn from my mistake. Of course, this story has a happy ending. The president of the company was so impressed with my show of integrity that the company sent me all of its litigation for years after.

I don't screw up much, of course, but I can give you another important example of taking responsibility for our bargains. I referred a case to a very good lawyer in Chicago. Before the statute of limitations ran out, I called this lawyer to see what the status of my client's case was. The lawyer assured me he would be filing a lawsuit that very week. Well, to make a long story short, he screwed up. He mailed the papers to the court on time, but the clerk sent them back because a form was not filled out properly. By the time it was actually filed, the statute was blown and my client's rights were forfeited.

My lawyer friend has malpractice insurance to handle mistakes like this one, and he promptly informed his insurer of the problem. He sent a letter to the client, taking full responsibility, and he called me to let me know. Another lawyer might have tried to hide the mistake. I was not too happy to get his call telling me he screwed up, but I would have been a whole lot less happy to find out from my client or by some other means. I respected that the lawyer took responsibility for his mistakes.

The only thing to do when we make a mistake is to take responsibility and make good on the promise as best we can. One mistake, one bad bargain, will not break us. It may seem monumental and awful. I'm sure the lawyer felt like poop when he realized his mistake. And I'm sure calling me to tell me was not something he relished, but he did the right thing, and I appreciated it. The client wasn't even mad because the lawyer made good by turning the matter over to his malpractice insurer. These things happen.

Make things as right as you can whenever you can, and let others do right by you, too. If you take your clothes to a cleaner and they ruin them, let them do right by you by replacing the wrecked items. If you accidentally break your neighbor's vase, replace it. If your neighbor breaks your vase, let her do the right thing and then move on. Give people second chances, just as you would hope to be given another chance yourself. If you give someone a chance to make things right, and he doesn't, then you can take appropriate action, whether it is suing or never doing business there again, or terminating a friendship. If we would all do the right thing (when we know what the right thing to do is), we would have long-lasting and productive relationships.

When we master the art and science of negotiation, we master life.

4

Ask What Your Country (and State and Village) Can Do for You

(HOW TO GET THE GOVERNMENT TO DO YOUR LEGAL WORK FOR FREE)

You pay taxes. Boy, do you pay taxes! You pay income tax, of course, and sales tax. You pay property taxes and gasoline taxes. You may pay corporate taxes if you own a business. You pay a "sin" tax if you smoke or drink. You pay hotel taxes and restaurant taxes and airline taxes when you travel. Those nice government people never stop thinking of ways to help you contribute to their support. Where does your money go? Mostly it goes to pay for government bureaucracy. But has it ever occurred to you that you can put that bureaucracy to work for you? I didn't think so. Government assistance programs aren't just for welfare recipients any more!

Whatever your income, I doubt that attorney's fees are part of your budget. Instead, you can get the government to do your legal work for free! Many branches of government exist just to help you. The government's help is not dependent on your income. It's available to everybody. It costs the taxpayers plenty, but it costs the user nothing. So how do you get what you've already paid for? Ask and ye shall receive.

Think Local

You picked the community you live in for a lot of reasons. Good schools? Great library? Low crime? These things don't just happen magically. They take careful planning and action by the people in charge—the people you elect to spend the money you send by way of your tax payments. They have an interest in keeping the town livable and keeping property values up, just like you do. So, they have created a system to make life in town run smoothly.

Let's say your next-door neighbor puts up a really *ugly* twelve-foot high fence on the property line that separates his homestead from yours. So, instead of looking out your kitchen window and seeing sunflowers and squirrels, you now see nothing but an ugly twelve-foot fence. In most towns, including the one I live in, ugly twelve-foot fences are illegal. We have codes, also known as ordinances, that dictate the height and materials which are allowed for residential area fences. So do I sue my neighbor for putting up an ugly fence? I could. I might sue for nuisance. I could spend money for filing fees and service of process. I could hire a lawyer, or I could do it myself, but then I'd have to miss time from work to go to court. And what if I won? There might be an appeal. What if the neighbor says the ordinance is unconstitutional? I like my house and I like my neighborhood. I don't like the fence, but I don't want to go bankrupt protecting my right not to have to look at it.

Lucky for me, my village, just like every other town and city and village in the country, has a department of code enforcement. I can call and say, "Hey! My dopey neighbor put up an ugly twelve-foot-high wooden fence on our property line. Can he *do* that?" If nothing else, I will find out whether or not he can do that. Chances are the code enforcement people will know the answer to my question without even looking it up. My neighbor is probably not the first guy in town to have the brilliant idea to put up an ugly twelve-foot fence, and I am not likely the first person in town to complain about one.

So if the code enforcement people say, "Nope. He can't do that. It violates the Fence Code," then what? Well, ask the code enforcement people. Probably they will send someone out to see the fence. They will file a complaint and issue some sort of ticket or compliance notice. This varies with the town, but all towns enforce their ordinances. There is always some procedure for handling code violations. The government will do it, and it won't cost you a cent. If your town sends your neighbor a letter, with a copy of the code, saying, "You have ten business days to take down your fence," then if the fence is still standing eleven days later, the town will take legal action. Usually there is a fine involved. The government attorney will prosecute the case in court. Eventually, the fence will probably come down. You get the outcome you wanted, but without any cost to you.

What else can your local government do for you? Let's say you rent. Tenants as a group probably call lawyers more often than anyone else. Sometimes people are renting because they can't afford to own a home. This also may mean they can't afford to hire a lawyer to sue their landlords. So if the landlord isn't providing heat, what's a tenant to do? Call the bureaucrats at city hall! Chances are the city has a requirement that landlords provide heat to their tenants. In Chicago, they actually set specific temperature requirements for both daytime and nighttime. Every winter, the Housing Department of the city is on the news telling people to call their hotline if they don't have heat. *Do it.* That's what it's there for. The town I used to live in had a Landlord-Tenant Liaison which helped resolve disputes between landlords and tenants relative to everything from rent disputes to vermin.

How do you know what resources are available from your municipality? Ask! Ideally, every city, town, and village would have a pamphlet to give every resident, which would list all the resources available from the government, along with names of contact people. My town has something called "Contacts for Your Assistance" that lists only the numbers for the Health Department, Zoning, Planning, et cetera. It's better than nothing, but they could do better. Find out if your local government has a directory of services. If so, get one, and keep it with your phone books. If not, encourage them to create one. You do pay taxes, after all, and you are entitled to know what you get for your money.

If you have a problem that you think the local government might be able to help with, call and find out. If you don't know which department to ask for, start with the mayor's office or the office of the town manager. The people who answer the phones there understand the local government. They can refer you to the proper people. If there are local resources outside of the town government, like a township or county office or a local charity, they can refer you there, too. If you are worried about your elderly neighbor who has no one to check on her, you can call the village. They will let you know if someone from the health department can go out and pay a visit. The possibilities are endless. The government will *never* come to you bearing gifts. You must go to the government. It's not charity; you're entitled. You're just getting what you paid for.

In my case, I pay a lot of local taxes. I own two homes in the same community. I have no kids who go to school and I have never needed much from the village. I don't mind paying the taxes. I like living in a town with good schools. Our local library is one of the best in the state. I've never had to use any village services until recently. The garbage trucks started coming at 6:15 in the *morning*. And these garbage trucks don't make just a little noise, and they don't make it for just a few minutes. They make so much noise they rattle my bedroom windows for ten minutes. I don't care to wake up at 6:15. So I called the mayor's office. "Don't we have any noise ordinances?" I asked. Yes, I was told. Garbage pickup cannot start before 7 A.M. So I told them about my garbage people coming at 6:15, which is punishable in our town by a five-hundred-dollar fine.

The mayor's office contacted the garbage company. They said they don't let their trucks out of the lot before seven, and so I must be mistaken. *So*, the next morning, I took pictures of the garbage truck picking up at 6:15. It was pitch black out except for the light in one window across the street. I signed a complaint against the company and the village prosecuted the garbage company. We went to court and the refuse company was fined one thousand dollars and put on supervision for a year. Best of all, they don't wake me up at 6:15 anymore. Otherwise I'd be too tired to write this book.

The State of the States

States are the biggest resource when it comes to getting legal help for free. Under the United States Constitution those functions of government not expressly given to the federal government are reserved to the states. There are many places to find lists of state government resources. All of them are available at your local library. Sometimes you will find lists of numbers for state offices in the government section of your local phone book. There are also phone books of state government offices available at the library. Many lawyers' resources list government offices. In Illinois we have a Law Directory which lists all the lawyers in Illinois and also lists phone numbers for state and federal offices and some city and county offices. I understand that every state has a similar volume but they are called by different names. Ask your librarian.

In Illinois we also have a valuable resource called *The Lawyer's Handbook*. Every lawyer has this little book on her desk. It costs about five dollars and is published by the same company that puts out our daily legal newspaper. It lists numbers for all the court clerks, county clerks, and state and federal offices. I asked at my local library if they have a copy of this book and I was told no, but they would like to have one. (By the time you read this book my local library will have one.) If you have a problem you think your state government should be able to help you with, call or visit your local library and get the appropriate office number to call. If your state has an affordable book listing government offices, by all means buy it. I have found offices in *The Lawyer's Handbook* I didn't know existed and I have used those offices to get help for myself and for my clients. Sometimes seeing a list of resources will help you get an idea of where to turn for help in solving your particular problem.

Most professionals are licensed by the state. Doctors are licensed. Teachers are licensed, and so are nurses. Even barbers and beauticians are licensed by the state. In some states, tattoo artists are licensed. So let's say you have a problem with a licensed professional. For example, you've decided to change doctors and your old doctor refuses to send your medical records to your new doctor. What do you do? Well, you could hire a lawyer and you could sue the doctor for a mandatory injunction requiring her to turn over the records. *Or* you could write to your state's Department of Professional Regulation. The name of this licensing bureau might differ slightly from state to state. If you check a list of government offices and you can't find something that resembles this name, call your library and ask which government office licenses doctors or barbers or tattoo artists, as the case may be.

Usually the government licensing office will not get money for you, but they will get the results you want. No doctor is willing to lose his medical license and his livelihood to deprive you of your medical records. Not to mention that while the state will pursue your claims at no cost to you, the doctor will probably need to hire a lawyer to defend him during any disciplinary proceeding. Educate yourself about the proper channels for making disciplinary complaints against doctors in your state. Sometimes a letter or fax to the doctor starting with "If I don't have my medical records by Monday I will file a complaint with the Illinois Department of Professional Regulation" will get you your records. If not, by all means file the complaint. It may take a while, but you will get your records. Bureaucracies are notoriously slow-moving. If you need your medical records and it is an emergency, then call the state and ask if there is some emergency procedure for expediting claims. If not, you may need to take the step of hiring a lawyer and filing an emergency lawsuit.

Similarly, if the local tattoo parlor puts a permanent pair of lips on your minor daughter's butt without your permission, you might want to file a complaint with the state. You might want to sue, too, but at least losing a license will keep the tattoo artist from tattooing any other teeny-bopper butts. Not all states license tattoo artists. Just keep in mind that you should check to see what the state can do to help you, if anything.

You can even file complaints against your lawyer! Every state has an attorney licensing agency. In Illinois it is called the Attorney Registration and Disciplinary Commission, also known as the ARDC. This commission answers to the Supreme Court of Illinois, and it issues licenses to lawyers. It can also discipline lawyers, including suspension and disbarment. If you tell an Illinois attorney that you are filing a complaint with the ARDC, she will pay you some attention. If you don't know who licenses lawyers in your state, ask a lawyer, or ask your library. Most important, if you have a complaint against a lawyer, *don't* call the local bar association. Bar associations are like country clubs. Membership in these organizations is voluntary. Bar associations provide services to lawyers; they do not discipline or license lawyers. Call the proper *government* office.

What other kinds of problems can your state government help you with? Let's say you get fired from your job. You probably know you can go apply for unemployment. But what if your employer owes you money? Should you sue? What if it's a small amount? Is it worth it to take the company to small claims court? Well, you could. But a better alternative would be to contact your state's Department of Labor. Under the law, you have an obligation to "exhaust your administrative remedies," which simply means that if there is a way to resolve a dispute through a government agency, you have to try.

The law of your state may or may not require you to seek relief of a wage dispute through the Department of Labor, but you may as well start there. It's free, and the people who work there deal with wage disputes for a living. If you're lucky you will only have a wage problem once. They know what your rights are better than you do. Not only that, but you may learn you are entitled to money you didn't know you had coming. If you work for a company for eleven months and get fired, you may not think you have any vacation pay coming, especially if your company's policy is that employees only earn vacation time after one year. *Don't rely on your boss, or former boss, to tell you what your rights are.* If your company grants two weeks vacation after one year, and you are fired after eleven months, you are entitled to pro-rated vacation pay 11/12ths of two weeks of pay. You will also be entitled to

COBRA benefits for health insurance from your employer's health insurance provider. The Department of Labor will help you get what you have coming.

How do you make a claim with your state's Department of Labor? Usually via a form. It asks who your employer or former employer is, how long you worked there, and what your rate of pay is. The Department of Labor will contact your employer and then conduct an investigation and hold a hearing before an administrative law judge. You may have an attorney present at the hearing if you like, but you certainly don't need one. If your employer owes you money, the law is on your side. Usually, awards of back wages by the Department of Labor are enforceable by a state's criminal statutes, and employers who fail to pay an award of back wages will be subject to criminal prosecution. It's some powerful stuff, and it's all on *your* side!

What if your employer discriminates against you? The law will protect you against discrimination based on your race, religion, sex, age, disability, marital status, and sometimes sexual orientation. If you suspect you are the victim of discrimination and you are a member of one of these groups, referred to as a "protected class," call your state's Department of Human Rights. Again, it might have a different official name, but the purpose will be the same. You might be surprised at the kinds of discrimination that qualify for assistance from the state. One case that surprised me involved a married woman working for a local travel agency. The agency provided health insurance benefits to its single women employees, but no health insurance to its married women employees. One of the owners was a man, but none of the employees were male. The employers' rationale in denying health insurance to the married women was that these women were covered on their husband's policies, and the agency thought it would save money this way, which, of course, it did. One married woman needed a hysterectomy, which she had, at considerable expense.

She was covered by her husband's health insurance policy, but his policy had a one-thousand-dollar deductible. If she had been covered on the agency's plan, she would have saved seven-hundred-fifty dollars, because their policy had only a two-hundred-fifty-dollar deductible. Covering one class and not another is discriminatory, and so she filed a claim with the Illinois Department of Human Rights—and won.

As a consumer, your best overall resource is your state's attorney general. Here is a list of some divisions of the Illinois Attorney General:

Agricultural Law

Antitrust

Asbestos Litigation

Charitable Trusts

Citizen's Rights

Civil Appeals

Commerce Commission

Communications

Condemnations and Land
    Acquisitions

Consumer Protection

Court of Claims

Crime Victims

Criminal Appeals

Criminal Prosecutions

Disabled Persons Advocacy

Environmental Control

Franchise

General Law

Government Representation

Hearing Impaired

Industrial Commission

Information Services

Inheritance Tax

Intergovernmental Relations

Investigations

Legislative Affairs

Medicaid Provider Fraud

Nursing Home Patient Abuse

Opinions

Personnel

Program Development and
    Evaluation

Public Aid

Public Interest Litigation

Public Service Intake Center

Public Utilities

Revenue Litigation

Senior Citizens Advocacy

Veterans Advocacy

Welfare Litigation

Pretty impressive list, huh? I hope that just reading this list will make you realize the endless possibilities for government help. If someone is dumping waste in your neighborhood, either on land or in water, call the Attorney General Environmental Control Department. If you suspect a charity that solicits funds from you is operating fraudulently, or if you just want to check out a charity, call your Attorney General's Department of Charitable Trusts. Two important divisions of your state's attorney general's office can protect you in consumer transactions and assist you if you are the victim of a crime. I've described them here so you will know when to call them for help.

Department of Consumer Protection

Hey, *you* are a consumer, and you certainly want protection! Many, many times, if you are scammed—by a contracting business, by a retail store that does not have the merchandise it advertises (called "bait and switch"), or any time you don't get what you pay for—the attorney general's office may be able to help you. Keep in mind that an attorney general is most interested in pursuing cases in which a pattern of abuse takes place. If you hire a man to clean your pool and he does a shabby job, the attorney general isn't going to care much. If the job is so bad that it constitutes a breach of your contract with the pool man, then take him to small claims court. If, on the other hand, you pay money to join a pre-paid legal plan, and when you need a lawyer you discover their number is disconnected, call your state's attorney general. You are probably not the only one in your state affected. It is far easier and more cost effective, especially when you are part of a group that has been defrauded, to let the state hunt down the perpetrators than it would be to file a small claim action on your own behalf. It would be difficult for the sheriff to serve papers on the people responsible, especially when you are not sure where to find them.

Crime Victim Assistance

Let's say you are hit by a drunk driver and injured. If the drunk goes to jail for the crime but has no insurance and no assets, there may be no point in suing him. If your state has a Crime Victims' Assistance Fund, you may be eligible for financial aid from the state. It is worth making a phone call and finding out.

Also, if you or someone you love is in a nursing home and being abused, you should contact the police *and* the state's attorney general. If there is no specific number for nursing home abuse, then call the main number and see if someone there can help you. If a person is injured as a result of abuse, the nursing home may be prosecuted by the state but you can also sue them for damages in civil court. But if the abuse is more subtle—not enough heat, or malnutrition—then call the attorney general. Chances are if they don't have a specific office to help you, they can refer you to another state office that can help.

Following are three other state offices of which you should be aware.

Department of Insurance

Call this agency if you have a problem with your insurance company. The Department of Insurance is not a small claims court, so if you are in a fender-bender and the insurance company offers you less for your car than you think it is worth, then the Department of Insurance will probably not help you. Check your policy for resolution of disputes. Usually the policy will require disputes between the insured and the company to be arbitrated. But what if your insurance company operates in bad faith? What if you get sued for an injury on your property and your home-owner's insurance carrier refuses to defend you in court? You can sue your insurance company. This is called a Declaratory Judgment action. You ask the court to declare that the insurance company owes you a duty. You can also contact the Department of Insurance and it will investigate. The Department of Insurance will also handle claims against bankrupt insurance companies.

Department of Revenue

This office can help you with tax problems. I will give you an example that may sound silly to you, but it shows how the Illinois Department of Revenue came through. Many of the gas stations in my area were charging eight percent tax on food. In Illinois, we have eight percent sales tax on general merchandise and two percent on food. When I was charged eight percent on food at various gas stations, I asked why. I was told their cash registers could only integrate one tax rate and so they charged eight percent tax on everything. Okay, we're not talking about a lot of money on an individual snack purchase—a bag of chips for a dollar would result in a six cent overcharge to the customer. However, total the snack purchases for a day or a week or a year and those extra taxes really add up. *Plus*, none of the gas stations that overcharged me on the tax would give me a receipt. So they might not have been reporting my cash purchases *or* the tax to the state. I reported these gas stations to the Illinois Department of Revenue; they were all "busted" and they all now charge the correct tax. Departments of Revenue handle all tax issues, so anytime you have questions or concerns about your state income tax or other state tax issues, call them.

Industrial Commission (Workers' Compensation)

Again, other states may call this kind of agency the Workers' Compensation Bureau or something similar. In the old days (before you and I were born) employees could sue their employers when they were injured at work. Apparently the courts were backlogged because so many employees were suing their employers. So there was a compromise, and now *anytime* an employee is injured at work, she is entitled to workers' compensation, whether the injury was the employer's fault, the employee's fault, or nobody's fault at all. The trade-off is that with a very few exceptions you can no longer sue your employer for the injury.

Workers' compensation is a state program. So, if you are injured at work, the benefits you are entitled to will depend on the state in which are employed and where you are injured. For example, in Illinois you would be entitled to two-thirds of your average weekly wage for as long as a doctor said you could *not* work; you would be entitled to have your medical bills paid one hundred percent as long as they were related to the work injury; and you might be entitled to an award of "permanent partial disability" to compensate you for the trauma that was sustained to your body. The Illinois Industrial Commission has a handbook that explains the rights of all injured workers in Illinois. Other states have similar handbooks for injured workers. If you are injured at work, find out your rights *immediately*.

What Is This? A *Federal* Case?

I always tend to think local before expanding my search for help. Why? Because the smaller the jurisdiction of the person or agency from whom you are seeking help, the more accountable they are to you. If you call the mayor of your city and ask for help, you are one of possibly thousands of constituents—and voters. If you call the President of the United States for help, he will have better things to do, he will think you are a nut, and the CIA will probably open a "permanent file" on you, which is not a good thing.

That said, the federal government's bureaucracy is unrivaled in the world. There are departments and agencies for just about every concern you can think of, from roads to drugs to smuggling, and then some. How do you go about making claims with the federal government? There is a reason government bureaucrats are said to be "buried in paper." Usually, in order to make any kind of complaint or get any kind of aid from the federal government, or any government agency, you will need to fill out forms. Some agencies prefer people who have complaints go into their offices and be interviewed—and fill out forms. Other agencies will send you a form. Call your local office of the agency from which you are seeking help, and I can guarantee the person who answers the phone will be able to tell you how that particular agency does business.

The offices of the federal government that are most associated with helping people are Medicare and Social Security. These two groups are commonly associated with the elderly. Everyone who works knows that these organizations exist to take money from our paychecks and take care of us when we get old. But many people do not know that Social Security and Medicare might be available to them or someone they care about who is disabled prematurely. If a woman has a burst aneurysm or was in a car accident and so cannot work, she might be entitled to Social Security income, even if she is young. If you know a disabled person who cannot make ends meet, have her contact the Social Security Administration.

What other agencies of the federal government might you look to for help?

The Equal Employment Opportunity Commission (EEOC)

This agency has offices in most cities. The EEOC investigates cases of employment discrimination or harassment based on age, gender, religion, race, marital status, and disability. The agency only involves itself in disputes against employers with fifteen or more employees, so keep that in mind. The agency will act as your advocate at no cost to you, and you need not have been fired to call upon its services. The statement by a male boss to a female employee, "You have nice legs for an old broad," has been held by the EEOC to constitute sexual harassment. No woman should be made to feel uncomfortable by the sexual tenor of her workplace.

The United States Postal Inspection Service (USPIS)

The post office investigates all complaints having *anything* to do with the *mail*. Think about that. If someone solicits your business through the mail or sends you a contract through the mail or is supposed to send you merchandise through the mail but doesn't, put your local postal inspector on the case. There are 800 numbers for filing complaints with the Postal Inspection Service, as well as local numbers. Your local post office can give you the number to the USPIS office that is responsible for your area.

If you have been victimized by a mail scam, or if you have an elderly neighbor or family member who keeps sending money to a bogus charity because of promises of big sweepstakes awards, call a postal inspector. The USPIS deals with fraud and also with other mail complaints like lost or stolen mail. They have forms that you can request and send in, and in my experience, a postal inspector will come out to your home or office when they are conducting their investigation. These individuals have many resources available to them, and they are charged with protecting *you*. Let them. They can put tracers in mail and do all kinds of cool things like that. They set up stings at post office box locations when people send in money for merchandise never received. This is one useful organization to have in your corner, and they have all the force of the United States government behind them. When the USPIS catches a crook, the United States attorneys prosecute the case.

Where to Turn for Help

So how do you know which government office to call for help? Let's say you have reason to believe an international drug cartel is operating out of the house next door to yours. Should you call the FBI? The DEA? The FDA? ATF? I know—it's alphabet soup to you. My advice is to call your local police. They will provide you with the immediate protection you need, and they will refer your suspicions to the appropriate government agencies. The same suggestion applies anytime you feel criminally threatened. If you get a death threat by mail, you can contact the USPIS, but I would call my local police. They will arrive promptly to pick up the letter and determine whether you need protection. Then they can send the letter to the FBI for fingerprinting or handwriting analysis, if necessary. If you have a stalker, or are being harassed by phone, call your local police. You will get the quickest, most visible protection from your local police, and again, they can always refer your case to the state's attorney to seek an order of protection, or to another government agency. Your local police have more experience dealing with other government agencies than you do, so if you ever feel that your physical safety is threatened, call the police.

If you have a problem with a foreign country, nobody but the federal government can help you. So, if your kid disappears in Haiti while doing Peace Corps work, call the State Department.

Call the State Department if you are thinking about traveling to another country and you want to know if you should be concerned for your own safety. The State Department issues travel advisories for this purpose.

If you have a problem that involves interstate commerce, only the federal government can help you. For example, if you are disabled and need help maneuvering into and out of a plane and an airline refused to provide assistance, contact the Federal Aviation Administration.

Official Help

You elect people to represent you. They represent you at every level of government. You have a city mayor or village president. You may have an alderman or village trustees. You definitely have a state representative. You also have a representative and a senator to represent you in the United States Congress. You even have a governor and a president. All of these people represent you, and representing *you* is their *only* job. They are accountable *only* to you (and each of their other constituents). Some elected officials are volunteers and have no staffs. These people will listen to you and will allow your input on how they vote on important issues, but don't expect them to do much else on your behalf. They will be too busy juggling family, career, and the volunteer position of representing you.

Call the Mayor

At the local level, your best bet for getting free help from an elected official is the mayor (a village president is the same for our purposes). Every mayor has staff people who can be made to jump, and then to ask "How high?" when the mayor gives the say-so. All the departments of a city or village answer to the mayor. If you have a problem with unresponsiveness from your police or fire department, or if your garbage is not being collected on schedule, or if there are street signs missing in your subdivision, and you cannot get help from the responsible departments directly, call the mayor.

Depending on the size of your town, and the personality of your mayor, you may get to speak directly to the mayor. In the city of Chicago, you will probably be directed to an aide. Not to worry. Aides have the backing of the mayor. A call from "Ms. Smith in the Mayor's Office" to any department head in the city will warrant some attention. Don't worry that only the heavy-hitter campaign contributors will get attention from the mayor or her staff. Those big shots have the mayor's home number. The people in the office work for *you*. Mayors get the blame when things go wrong (if you don't believe me, ask *former* Mayor Mike Bilandic about the paralyzing blizzard of 1979 in Chicago), and they grab with gusto all the credit when things go right (like Rudy Giuliani and the lowered murder rate in New York City). If your local police are patronizing the crack house on your block that they are supposed to be busting, your mayor may want to hear about it. If stop signs are missing at a busy intersection, the mayor may want to know about that because if there are tragic consequences because of it, you-know-who will be taking the blame.

Call Your Congressman!

Until I started working on this book I never thought of how many different problems my congressman can help me solve. It was only when I called my congressman's office, just for *you*, to find out what kind of help you can get from *your* state's congressman, that I realized what a gold mine the congressman's office is. My congressman is John Porter. I hope you know who yours is, but if your don't, call your town hall and find out.

I called Congressman Porter's local district office. The district office has people in it whose only job is to help you. I reached a person named Mary Beth Hartmann, who is a staffer in Mr. Porter's district office, and I asked her, "Hi. I'm a constituent of Congressman Porter's. What can you help me with?" (If she thought I was a nut, she was polite and didn't say so.) To say that I was overwhelmed by the plethora of items Ms. Hartmann rattled off would be an understatement. Among other things, call your congressman's district office anytime you need help with any of these items:

IRS

Believe it or not, the IRS makes an occasional mistake. If the IRS makes a mistake on your taxes and you cannot come to a resolution of the problem by providing the appropriate documentation to the IRS, then try calling your congressman's office. At least they can look into it. Or say you are forming a nonprofit corporation and you can't figure out how to fill out all those 501[c](3) documents. Your congressman's office might be able to help.

Postal Service

The United States Postal Service is the most obvious federal agency. If you have problems with the mail, your congressman's office can look into it for you.

Student Loans

Many students are able to get educated only because of federal student loan programs. Your congressman can help you find available student loan funds and can also help you after you graduate, if you have problems with the repayment program. Student loan administrators make mistakes, like all of us, and like overworked bureaucrats do especially. Several years ago I got a small check and a letter from my student loan administrator telling me I had overpaid. Trust me—I did not overpay my student loan on purpose. I paid what they said I owed. If you have a problem with your student loan, call your congressman.

Housing

Federal housing programs, and especially "Section Eight" housing programs, exist to provide shelter to people who would otherwise be unable to obtain housing. Even in affluent districts, a congressmen's staff is more aware of the availability of federal housing dollars than the rest of us are. They also know of resources within their districts that are available to help their constituents in need.

Small Business Administration (SBA)

Many women who never thought of owning their own businesses are having their eyes opened to the opportunities of small business ownership. The federal government has many programs, including grants, to help people, and especially women, start and maintain small businesses. The SBA is the administrator of some of these programs. Your congressman's office can alert you to some of the available programs, and can help you get the government help you need for your business.

Social Security and Medicare

We all know someone we care about who collects Social Security and receives Medicare benefits. Both of these are huge federal programs with bureaucracies to match. So what to do if you are having a hard time resolving disputes with Social Security or Medicare? Call your congressman. By making a phone call, they can get more information for you than you could get yourself through hours of research.

Americans with Disabilities Act (A.D.A.)

Under the Americans with Disabilities Act, citizens with physical impairments are entitled to have reasonable accommodations in various settings, including places of employment, public transit, and public buildings. If you are disabled and you feel that you are not being given proper accommodation, you can sue, but you may be able to get the relief you are looking for by having your congressman intervene on your behalf instead.

Foreign Travel

If you have concerns related to travel outside of the United States, your congressman might be able to help you. Congressmen have been known to expedite the replacement of a lost passport. Their staffs can also look into the safety of foreign travel for you and provide you with the addresses of foreign consulates and embassies in the United States and also of American embassies in the countries to which you may be traveling.

If you have a loved one who is traveling abroad and encounters some difficulty, or if you lose contact with a family member who is overseas on vacation or business, your congressman might be able to help.

Immigration and Naturalization

If you are having immigration problems, call your congressman for sure. Sometimes employers will have foreign employees who have problems renewing their paperwork to stay in the United States. It can be disruptive to an employer if a staff person has to leave the country because of some bureaucratic snafu that results in an expired visa.

If you have a family member in another country whom you would like to have join you here in the United States, either permanently or on a short-term basis, your congressman might be able to help with required paperwork.

International Trade

If your business wants to open a branch in Beijing or import products from Penang, the bureaucracies at both ends can be daunting, especially if you are a newcomer to international trade. Your congressman's office can help expedite matters.

Federal Contracts

Not only is the federal government one of the largest employers there is, it is also one of the richest sources of contract work. Let's say you start up a road construction business or a painting business, and you want to do work for the federal government. Your congressman can help you find out what local contracts in your field are becoming available. They can also help you learn the bid process. Your congressman would rather see one of his constituents get a big federal contract than an outside firm.

Veterans and Military

Again, if you are a veteran, or if someone in your family is in the military, you might need the help of your congressman's office, either to identify existing services or to resolve issues. If your son came home from serving in a foreign country with some strange illness, your congressman can help trace whether your son was exposed to certain chemicals. He can also help your son obtain veteran's benefits such as medical care or disability pay.

Congressmen can help young people gain entry to the military academies. Your congressman can also help with questions about Selective Service registration and the G.I. Bill. It's also faster and more efficient to get an answer from your congressman's staff assistant than to call from government office to government office yourself.

Environmental Protection

You may find yourself on either side of an environmental dispute. You may learn there are gasoline tanks buried on your next door neighbor's property, or worse, you may learn there are gasoline tanks buried on your *own* property. You can bet there is a federal regulation that affects the removal of those tanks. Your congressman can help.

FCC and Internet

I found this hard to believe, but some people call their congressman about problems with their phone bills. Sometimes there are unidentifiable charges, including weird federal taxes. Sometimes people have their long-distance carriers changed without their permission. It would not have occurred to me to call my congressman about these issues, but because the Federal Communications

Commission regulates the telephone companies, your congressman's office can help you get answers. Also, because the Internet is relatively new in the scheme of things, there is not an established federal bureaucracy to handle concerns regarding the Internet. So if you have concerns or questions about the Internet, call your congressman.

Every Other Federal Thing

According to my congressman's office, they have seven full-time people in the various district offices just to handle constituent concerns. They do everything I have listed above and many things I haven't even thought of. They can get you tickets to federal tourist attractions, like the White House. They can get official flags for local Boy Scout troops and schools, the same ones that fly over the Congress on a daily basis. They can refer you to other government offices and agencies if they can't help you.

They can also do something else that is very important—they can represent your interests in regard to legislation. If a bill is pending in Congress and you have strong feelings about it, by all means, call your congressman. Alternately, if you feel a change in the law is needed, discuss it with your congressman. We are moving forward, for better or for worse, and sometimes the law does not keep up. If you have an idea how to make the country safer, smarter, more efficient, or simply more pleasant, and a law will help, call your congressman. I do not mean to minimize the possibilities, and I am not trying to be cute. Some very important laws have come about as a result of other people's tragedies. The Brady Bill, relating to gun ownership and registration, was named in honor of its instigator, Ronald Reagan's former Secret Service agent who was shot defending the president. Other laws are named for other citizens who thought, "Why can't we make this change for the better?" and suggested legislation to a congressman who proposed it. If you have an idea for a new law, call your congressman.

Call Your State Legislator!

No matter which state you live in, you have at least one legislator who represents you at the state level. Unlike a congressman, a state legislator (usually a state representative or state senator) cannot help you with federal issues. A state legislator cannot help you get a passport or a visa. A state legislator cannot solve a hostage situation in Iraq. *But* there is *some* overlap in the areas your congressman and state legislator can help you with, and there are also some areas in which your state legislator can help you and in which your congressman would be pretty useless.

For example, there are both federal and state programs for public aid. So both your congressman and your state legislator might be able to help you get aid if you need help feeding or housing your family. Also, sometimes states have programs that mirror federal programs, like those for employment discrimination and charity fraud. So if you have a problem along those lines, you can try getting help from either your congressman or your state legislator. Keep in mind that if you call the wrong place they will not shun you, they will merely refer you to the other's office. So if you call your congressman about getting help as a foster parent, she will probably refer you to your state legislator.

What areas can your state legislator help you with? Just like your congressman who can help you with any federal program, your legislator can help you with any state program. Public aid is a big one. Sometimes, even if the public aid dollars are federal money, the public aid programs are administered by the states, and so your legislator can help you get funding if you are qualified. Your state legislator can help you get special license plates for your car, because license plates are issued by the states.

Although a state legislator will refer you to your congressman for IRS tax problems, the legislator can help you with problems relating to your state's taxes. If you have questions or concerns about your driving privileges, your state legislator can help. Let's say your driving privileges are suspended for a period of time and you have a hard time getting your license reinstated; your state legislator can probably help. If you have problems with other licenses regulated by your state, call your legislator. If you move from Illinois to Texas and you are a nurse, you might have to have your license verified or transferred through reciprocity or you might have to be re-licensed. Licensing is a state process, so your state legislator can help you with it.

Most states have programs to help women collect child support. If you have children and you are owed child support, hiring a lawyer and dragging a deadbeat dad into court can be time-consuming and very expensive. For this reason, many women and children suffer economically because they don't know how to get affordable help. The states have an interest in helping every kid get support from both parents. Kids who are unsupported suffer economically, socially, and academically, and sometimes end up on public aid. So each state has a program to help collect child support. In Illinois, the various state's attorney's offices have programs to garnish the wages of unsupportive fathers. If you have a problem receiving child support, or if you just don't know where to turn, try your state legislator. They will uncover the various resources for you.

On the following pages I've included some of the forms that various government agencies will send you when you call to ask for help. These are just samples to give you an idea how the communication between you and your government will work. If you have a problem that your local, state, or federal government might be able to help you with, by all means call and get the right stuff.

MAIL FRAUD
COMPLAINT
QUESTIONNAIRE

Thank you for contacting the United States Postal Service concerning your complaint. To assist the U.S. Postal Inspection Service in handling this matter, please provide the following information.

Please return the completed form to your local post office.

A. Complainant information *(Please print or type)*:

1. Name: _____

2. Address: _____

   City: _____

   State: _____ ZIP Code: _____

3. Home Telephone: (   ) _____

4. Work Telephone: (   ) _____

B. Complaint against:

1. Company/Individual Name: _____

2. Address: _____

   City: _____

   State: _____ ZIP Code: _____

3. Telephone: (   ) _____

4. Name and title of person you dealt with: _____

   _____

C. First contact with company/individual was by:

1. ❑ U.S. Mail   When: _____

2. ❑ Telephone   When: _____

3. ❑ Newspaper/Magazine   Name: _____

4. ❑ Radio/TV   When: _____

5. ❑ Other, describe: _____

Additional comments: _____

_____

_____

D. Particulars of complaint:

1. Describe product/service offered: _____

_____

_____

_____

2. Was order made by: ❑ U.S. Mail

                              ❑ Telephone

                              ❑ Other, describe:

_____

3. Amount of money involved: _____

4. Was payment made by: ❑ Check

                              ❑ Money Order

                              ❑ Credit Card

                              ❑ Other, describe: _____

_____

_____

5. Date payment sent: _____

6. How was payment sent? ❏ Regular Mail

   ❏ Registered Mail

   ❏ Certified Mail

7. Was product/service received?

   If so, give date received:

8. How was it delivered? ❏ U.S. Mail

   ❏ COD

   ❏ UPS

   ❏ Other, describe: _____

   _____

   _____

9. Have you contacted company/individual about your complaint? ___

   If so, give date:_____

10. Did you request a refund? _____ If so, give date: _____

11. Did you receive a refund? _____ If so, give date: _____

12. Date of last contact with firm: _____

Additional Comments:

_____

_____

_____

_____

_____

Your signature: _____Date: _____

Please include copies of bills, receipts, advertisements, canceled checks (front and back) and any correspondence about this problem. (PLEASE DO NOT SEND ORIGINALS AT THIS TIME.)

As information, the U.S. Postal Inspection Service has no authority to effect refunds or adjustments, and there is no action we can take in this regard. However, under our Consumer Complaint Program we do contact individuals or businesses on behalf of the customer and request that complaints be resolved. As an investigative agency, it is our function to gather facts and evidence in order that a determination can be made as to whether action is warranted under the Mail Fraud or False Representation Statutes.

For your protection, we ask that you be very cautious in the future. Through our investigations we have found that people who have been victims of a fraud may be contacted again by the same fraud operator under another name or with a new scheme. We have also learned that the fraud operators also sell their mailing lists and frequently identify those people who were victimized, regardless of whether the victim complained or not.

Before conducting a business transaction, it is always a good idea to contact the Chamber of Commerce, The Better Business Bureau, or the county or state Office of Consumer Affairs in the geographical area where the firm is located to obtain whatever information they may be able to provide.

Thank you for bringing this matter to our attention.

POSTMASTERS: Please mail completed forms to the following address:

MANAGER, FRAUD AND PROHIBITED MAILINGS GROUP
U.S. POSTAL INSPECTION SERVICE
475 L'ENFANT PLAZA WEST, SW
WASHINGTON, DC 20260-2166

PS Form 8165, December 1993 (Page 4 of 4)

CHARGE QUESTIONNAIRE

EEOC Use Only	Name (Intake Officer)

This form is affected by the Privacy Act of 1974; see Privacy Act Statement on back before completing this form.

Please answer the following questions, telling us briefly why you believe you have been discriminated against in employment.

When was the most recent date the harm you are alleging took place? _____ (Date(s))

If you believe an employer discriminated against you, approximately how many employees does that employer have? _____ (Number)

(Please Print)

NAME _____ _____ _____
   (First)   (Middle Name or Initial)   (Last)

ADDRESS _____ _____ _____ DATE _____
   TELEPHONE NO. (Include area code)

CITY _____ STATE _____ ZIP _____ COUNTY _____

SOCIAL SECURITY NO. _____

Please provide the name of an individual at a different address in your local area who would know how to reach you.

NAME _____ RELATIONSHIP _____ PHONE _____

ADDRESS _____ CITY _____ STATE _____ ZIP _____

I believe I was discriminated against by the following employer(s) _____; labor union(s) _____; employment agency(ies) _____. (Check all that apply)

NAME _____

ADDRESS _____

NAME _____

ADDRESS _____

CITY, STATE, ZIP _____

PHONE NUMBER _____

CITY, STATE, ZIP _____

PHONE NUMBER _____

Are you now employed by the Employer that you believed discriminated against you?

YES: From _____   NO: I applied for _____   OR: I was employed as _____
            (date)   (position)   (position)

_____   on _____   until _____   I was _____
(current position)   (Date)   (date)   (laid off, fired, etc.)

Cause of discrimination based on (Check appropriate box(es)):

[ ] Race   [ ] Color   [ ] Sex   [ ] Religion   [ ] Age   [ ] Retaliation

[ ] National Origin   [ ] Disability   [ ] Other - Explain briefly:

What action was taken against you that you believe to be discriminatory? What harm, if any, was caused to you or others in your work situation as a result of that action? (if more space is required, use the next page.)

_____

_____

_____

_____

_____

_____

EEOC Form 283 (Test 10/94)

97

Attachment to Form 283

If you are filing a charge against an Employer, state the nature of the firm's business. (For example, Cleaning Service or Electronics Manufacturer.)

_____

What makes you believe that the action(s) occurred because of your (race, sex, national origin, religion, color, age, disability, <u>as applicable</u> <u>or</u> because or retaliation):

_____

_____

_____

_____

- and how will discrimination be proved?

Witnesses to action(s)?   YES [ ]   NO [ ]

Comparators?   Are there others of different (race, sex, national origin, religion, color, age and/or disability <u>as applicable</u>) treated more favorably than you under similar circumstances?

                            YES [ ]   NO [ ]

Are there others of the same (race, sex, national origin, religion, color, age and/or disability as applicable) who are treated more favorably than you under similar circumstance?

YES [ ]   NO [ ]

Biased remarks, gestures, etc., (describe): _____

_____

_____

_____

_____

Other proof of discrimination: _____

_____

_____

_____

_____

Continuation from page 1:

_____
_____
_____
_____
_____
_____
_____
_____
_____
_____
_____
_____
_____

Normally, your identity as a complainant will be disclosed to the organization which allegedly discriminated against you.

Do you [ ] consent or [ ] not consent to such disclosures?

Have you filed a complaint about the action you think was discriminatory with any other Federal, State, or Local Government Anti-discrimination agency?

[ ] No [ ] Yes (If answer is yes, complete below.)

100

NAME OF SOURCE ASSISTANCE _____

RESULTS IF ANY: _____   DATE _____

Have you sought assistance about the action you think was discriminatory from any other agency, from your union, an attorney, or from any other source? ☐ No ☐ Yes (If answer is yes, complete below.)

NAME OF SOURCE ASSISTANCE _____

RESULTS IF ANY: _____   DATE _____

Have you filed an EEOC Charge in the past? ☐ No ☐ Yes (if answer is yes, complete below)

| APPROX. DATE FILED | ORGANIZATION CHARGED | CHARGE NUMBER (IF KNOWN) |

I declare under penalty of perjury that the foregoing is true and correct.

SIGNATURE _____   DATE _____

101

DANIELS PRINTING & OFFICE SUPPLY — OAK FOREST · IL 60452   301637-DQ

WAGE CLAIM APPLICATION
Illinois Department of Labor
160 N. LaSalle Street, Ste. C-1300
Chicago, Illinois 60601
(312) 793-2808

PLEASE PRINT OR TYPE ALL INFORMATION
Use additional sheets if necessary. Attach copies of all supporting documentation and
other evidence. A copy of this claim will be sent to the employer.

FOR OFFICE USE ONLY
Wage Claim Number _____

PRINT OR TYPE ALL INFORMATION IN INK. PRESS HARD...YOU ARE MAKING 3 COPIES.

CLAIMANT INFORMATION:

Your Name _____

Address _____

City, State _____ Zip _____

Social Security # _____ [ ] Male [ ] Female

Home Telephone ( )_____

Current Work Telephone ( )_____

EMPLOYER INFORMATION:

Business Name _____

Address _____

City, State _____ Zip _____

Corporation Name, if any _____

Contact Name _____

Phone Number ( )_____

1. Who hired you? _____ 2. Supervisor Name _____ 3. # of Employees _____

4. Did you sign an employment contract or agreement? [ ] Yes (attach copy) [ ] No   5. Did your employer set regular working hours? [ ] Yes   [ ] No

6. Was the employer's business [ ] Retail [ ] Manufacturing [ ] Construction [ ] Other (explain) _____

7. What type of work did you perform? _____

8. Address where work was done: _____

9. Were you an independent contractor? [ ] Yes [ ] No   Do you own a business? [ ] Yes [ ] No   If yes, type of business: _____

10. What was your rate of pay? Hourly $_____ Weekly $_____ Monthly $_____ Other (explain) _____

11. Was your rate of pay agreement: [ ] Oral [ ] Written (Attach a copy)   12. How often were you paid? [ ] Weekly [ ] Bi-Weekly [ ] Monthly

[ ] Semi-Monthly [ ] Other (explain) _____

13. Are you still working for this employer? [ ] Yes [ ] No   Is the company still in operation? [ ] Yes [ ] No

102

14. Did you quit? [ ] Yes [ ] No   Were you discharged? [ ] Yes [ ] No   Other (explain) _____

15. Date hired _____ Last day worked _____   16. Were you in a union? [ ] No [ ] Yes (Name/Local #) _____

17. Total amount of claim (do <u>not</u> deduct taxes or social security) $ _____   18. Is the claim for unpaid: [ ]¹Wages $ _____

[ ]²Vacation Pay $ _____   [ ]³Bonus Pay $ _____   [ ]⁴Commissions $ _____   [ ]⁵Illegal Deductions $ _____   [ ]⁶Other $ _____

19. If you claim WAGES, dates for which wages were not paid: _____   Number of hours worked and not paid: _____

at $ _____ per hour. If salaried rather than hourly, number of days/weeks/months not paid _____ at $ _____ per _____

20. If you claim VACATION PAY, does the employer have a policy? [ ] Yes (If yes, explain fully or attach copy) [ ] No

List vacations covered, taken, and paid during your employment with the employer:

Period Worked (Mo/Day/Year) to (Mo/Day/Year)		No. Days/Weeks Earned	Dates Taken	Dates Paid
From: _____	to _____	_____	_____	_____
From: _____	to _____	_____	_____	_____
From: _____	to _____	_____	_____	_____

21. If you claim BONUS pay, what was the bonus formula? Attach copy of any written policy or agreement. Explain how you arrived at the amount

of your claim: _____

22. If you claim COMMISSIONS, what was the commission formula? Attach copy of any written policy or agreement. What was the total amount of

sales, etc. on which commissions were not paid? _____ Attach an itemization of each sale, etc. to this application.

23. If you claim ILLEGAL DEDUCTIONS, explain why the deduction(s) was (were) made: _____

Did you authorize the deduction(s) in writing? [ ] Yes [ ] No

24. If you claim OTHER, explain how you arrived at the amount of your claim. If company benefit, attach a copy of the written policy, or, if unwritten,

explain fully: _____

I HEREBY CERTIFY that the foregoing including attachments, is true and accurate to the best of my knowledge and belief. I UNDERSTAND that
acceptance of this claim by the Illinois Department of Labor does not guarantee collection. I AUTHORIZE the Department of Labor to receive any
monies and to mail such monies to me at my own risk.

Date _____   Claimant's Signature _____

BLUE COPY = DEPARTMENT COPY; YELLOW COPY = EMPLOYER COPY; PINK COPY = CLAIMANT COPY

Jim Ryan
ILLINOIS ATTORNEY GENERAL

CONSUMER COMPLAINT FORM

| CTS NO. |
| REGIONAL NO. |
| CATEG. CODE: |

Revised: January 1994

1. Please to be sure to complain to the company or individual before filing.
2. Please type or print clearly in dark ink.
3. Incomplete or unclear forms will be returned to you.
4. Make sure you enclose copies of important papers concerning your transaction.

CONSUMER:

Your Name	Senior Citizen? ☐ Yes ☐ No	Day Tel.
Street Address		Night Tel.
City/Town	State	Zip

COMPLAINT:

| Name of Seller or Provider of Services | Name of Other Seller or Provider of Services |

Street Address

City/Town

State	Zip	Telephone

Date of Transaction

Cost of Product

Street Address

City/Town

State	Zip	Telephone

How Paid

Did you sign a contract?
☐ Yes ☐ No Where? _____ Date _____

Was product or service advertised?
☐ Yes ☐ No Where? _____ Date _____

Type of Complaint—e.g. car, mail order, etc. (Use reverse to provide details):

Have you complained to the company or the individual?
☐ Yes ☐ No How? ☐ By Mail ☐ By Telephone ☐ In person Date _____

Person Contacted

Job Title

Nature of Response

Date of Response

Has matter been submitted to another agency or attorney? ☐ Yes ☐ No If yes, give name and address:

Is court action pending?
☐ Yes ☐ No

105

FILL OUT IF COMPLAINT IS ABOUT A MOTOR VEHICLE OR APPLIANCE:

Make	Model		Year	VIN or Serial Number	
Purchased ☐ New ☐ Used	Sold ☐ With Warranty ☐ As Is		Warranty Expiration Date	Purchase Date	Mileage

MISCELLANEOUS:

Briefly describe your complaint:

What form of relief are you seeking? (e.g. exchange, repair, money back, etc.)

106

Who referred you to this office?

READ THE FOLLOWING BEFORE SIGNING BELOW:

PLEASE ATTACH TO THIS FORM **PHOTOCOPIES** of any papers involved (contracts, warranties, bills received, cancelled checks - front and back, correspondence, etc.) **DO NOT SEND ORIGINALS.**

In order to resolve your complaint we may send a copy of this form to the person or firm you are complaining about.

In filing this complaint, I understand that the Attorney General is not my private attorney, but represents the public in enforcing laws designed to protect the public from misleading or unlawful business practices. I also understand that if I have any questions concerning my legal rights or responsibilities, I should contact a private attorney. I have no objection to the contents of this complaint being forwarded to the business or person the complaint is directed against. The above complaint is true and accurate to the best of my knowledge.

Signature: _____   Date: _____

HAVE YOU ENCLOSED COPIES OF IMPORTANT PAPERS?

RETURN TO: **Jim Ryan, Attorney General**
Consumer Protection Division
100 West Randolph Street
Chicago, Illinois 60601
(312) 814-3000

 Printed on Recycled Paper

107

5

Talk Is Cheap, and So Is Paper

(HOW TO WRITE EFFECTIVE LETTERS)

Everybody knows that talk is cheap. Sometimes, talk can also be effective, so it's usually worth a try when you're attempting to solve a problem. However, a letter is often a more effective way to get satisfaction, make things right, change someone's mind, or resolve a dispute. But not just any old dashed-off letter will get results. It's got to be the right letter.

Persuasion vs. Extortion

There is a very slim but definable line between persuasion and extortion. Take the notorious case involving Autumn Jackson and Bill Cosby. Jackson went to prison for attempting to extort money from Bill Cosby.

She believed Cosby was her father because her mother told her so. Jackson believed her mother because Cosby had been part of her life for quite some time. He'd even paid her a few thousand dollars here and there—*but not* child support. Additionally, Jackson's mother had an affair with Cosby about the time she was conceived. So Jackson demanded money from Cosby. Because of this, she was convicted of extortion.

It seems to be the general public consensus that prison was too good for Jackson. Many lawyers and reporters have said that it was irrelevant whether Cosby was, in fact, her father. It doesn't seem irrelevant to me at all. In most states, 20 percent of a man's net income is standard child support for one child. If a man makes many millions of dollars a year, then this child support responsibility would, over several years, amount to many millions of dollars.

Autumn Jackson spent time in prison for doing what I've been doing—legally—for a living for fourteen years. If a young woman presented herself in my office and said that she believed a male celebrity was her father, enumerating several good reasons for believing so, I would have told her that if it was true and provable, she might be entitled to millions of dollars in retroactive child support. Any other good lawyer would have told her the same thing. The laws of the state in which the woman was conceived and the laws of the state in which the putative father and the woman reside could all determine what her rights were.

If I believed her—and I don't take clients unless I believe them—I would first write a letter to the prospective dad. It would say something like this:

Dear Mr. Celebrity:
My client, Ms. Offspring, has reason to believe that you are her father. If this is the case, you may owe her millions of dollars in retroactive child support. Please have your attorney contact me so that we may discuss the possibility of a pater-

nity test, or a settlement of this matter, as the case may be. If I do not hear from you or your attorney within fourteen days, we will be forced to take legal action against you, including a lawsuit. I am hoping this matter can be amicably resolved to the benefit of all parties. Thank you for your attention and cooperation.

Sincerely,
Margaret M. Basch
World's Greatest Lawyer

Mr. Celebrity's lawyer might insist on a paternity test, and I would advise my client to consent. The matter might be closed at that point. Or Mr. Celebrity might have decided against a paternity test and refused to discuss the matter further. Many scenarios are possible. One likely result would have been a lawsuit. However, if I had threatened on my letterhead to file a lawsuit for retroactive child support, no one would have accused me of extortion. But Autumn Jackson went to prison for doing what people pay me to do for them on my letterhead, every day. Her real crime may have been not hiring a lawyer.

It is my job as an effective advocate to suggest that litigation is always a possibility when discussions and negotiations fail. When a celebrity is involved, litigation often results in publicity. A good reputation has value in our society, and litigation can be damaging to a business, to a celebrity, or to any of us. It's a fact of life that some of us have more to lose than others.

Threatening a lawsuit is not generally considered extortion. If you have a claim because someone violated your rights, then writing a letter like the one above can often avoid costly litigation. When you really are in the right, the threat of a lawsuit, presented properly, is a form of "legal blackmail." Extortion, on the other hand, is the obtaining of property from another person or entity by threat of force, violence, fear, or under color of law.

That said, don't try to extort money illegally. Don't threaten anyone in writing. If you feel you have a claim, write a letter that suggests discussion, compromise, or resolution to avoid costly litigation.

Truth as a Defense

The other legal no-no in letter writing is defamation. A letter is defamatory if it's unjustly injurious to someone's reputation. Do not write a letter with untruthful and damaging information about an individual. The classic example from law school is stating that a person has a venereal disease. Truth is a defense, so if the person really *does* have syphilis, you're relatively safe.

Because injury to reputation is an essential element of defamation, only statements made to third parties are actionable. So if I write you a letter and call you a slut, there's not a lot you can do about it. If, however, I write to your neighbors, your employer, or your mother and tell them that you're a slut, then you can sue me. Moral turpitude is defamatory *per se*, unless, of course, it's true. A woman wrote to me once to tell me the reason my client won his case is that I slept with her lawyer. There's not a lot I can do about that. She also wrote to her own lawyer and accused him of sleeping with me. Again, since we both knew her statements to be untrue (and nutty), there was not a lot we could do about her statements. But she also wrote to the judge in the case and told him that she lost her case because I slept with her lawyer. Of course, the judge sent copies to me and my opposing counsel. I don't think he believed her statements, but I then had a case against the nutty woman for defamation.

Keep in mind that if you get sued for defamation, or anything else, it will cost you, even if you win. I have sued for defamation and won (see nutty woman story, above). I have also been sued for defamation and even though I won that, too, it cost me. My lawyers spent dozens of hours preparing a motion for summary judgment and I and several witnesses had to be presented for a deposition. Because the person who sued me is also an attorney, it didn't really cost him anything to sue me, and to drag out the case and to harass me, even though he surely knew he didn't have a case against me.

So be prudent when writing a letter about someone else. Ask yourself why you are doing it—if it's simply for revenge or for emotional reasons, don't do it—and what outcome you expect. And be sure to speak only the provable truth.

Never Put Anything in Writing You Don't Want the Whole World to Read

I don't want to deter anyone from writing tough action letters. One purpose of this chapter is to tell you how to do that, but please use due care. The written word has the potential to live forever. Listen to your instincts. I've shown my letters to a colleague with the query, "Is this too strong?" But the fact of the matter is, that letter is going out over my signature, and even if another lawyer tells me he thinks it's okay, I'm the one who has to live with the letter and its consequences. So make sure that the information, ideas, and assertions you put into a letter are ones you can stand by and live with for a long time.

If you tell your cousin Joe that your aunt Mabel is a lousy cook, it may or may not get back to her. You can always claim Joe misunderstood or misheard. "Mabel is a great cook," you can profess to have said, "but my mom will always be my favorite." Mabel will be appeased and you will be permitted entry to her future gatherings. If, on the other hand, you send your cousin Joe an email telling him that you and your clan were up all night sick because of Aunt Mabel's cooking and maybe she should learn some kitchen hygiene, you will be sunk with the family forever if Aunt Mabel lays eyes on your email.

We have all read stories about congressmen who wrote outrageous things in their youth on important issues, like whether drug use should be legal, and it came back to haunt them. Better that some pothead from the congressman's college days should tell Howard Stern, "Yeah, Joe used to say marijuana use among America's youth should be encouraged," than to see a reprint of a letter young Joe wrote to the editor of the *New York Times*, advocating exactly the same thing.

Pen to paper and keyboard to cyberspace are the modern-day equivalent, by the way. If you get into a "private" chat online and type "My husband is impotent" (or gay) do not assume it will not get back to him. People print or save emails, instant messages, even chat logs. So unless you are comfortable with your boss, parents, kids, spouse, friends, and strangers reading it, do not write it. By the way, the courts have held that your office email account is not private, and because your employer owns it your employer can read, print, and pass on your emails. Assume she will. If you are lucky, like me, some crazy cyberstalker or computer hacker will glom onto you and read your email from some remote location. Assume all your emails, both incoming and outgoing, will be read by additional eyes.

Writing Action Letters

I was once represented by a lawyer who made me do all my own work. Then he would say to me, "Wow, you write one hell of a letter." It's true. I do write great letters. After all, I'm the world's greatest lawyer. What did I need him for?

What's a great letter? It conveys your message, clearly and directly, without any extraneous stuff. This applies to every kind of letter there is. Take a love letter. What is the point? The message is "I love you." Every thing about "I love you" belongs in the letter. Other stuff does not. Know your audience, and know your bounds.

Action letters are unlike any other kind of letter there is. They don't necessarily express sentiment, like letters to loved ones; they demand action on the part of the recipient:

Dear Ms. So-and-So:

    I want you to do _____, and I want you to do it by _____. The reason I want you to take this action is _____, and if you don't do it, then the consequence will be _____.

Sincerely,
Ms. This-and-That

There. Now you know how to write an action letter. Here is an example, following the form:

1 June 2000
Mr. John Smith
Smitty's Roofing
My Town, USA 00000

Dear Mr. Smith:

    As I explained to you this morning, the new roof you installed on my house last month leaks when it rains. I expect you to come and repair the roof within seven days. You provided a one-year warranty against leakage (copy enclosed), and I expect you to make good on this warranty. If you do not, I will turn this matter over to my attorneys.

Sincerely,
Mary Homeowner

How simple is that? You might want to put a "cc" on the bottom of the letter, with your attorney's name on it, but if you do this, make sure your attorney is aware of it. Otherwise, your attorney might get a call from Mr. Smith's lawyer, your lawyer will look like a dope, and you will look like a liar.

Keep your letter as short and concise as possible. I once wrote a three-page letter of complaint, because there was so much wrong with the service I received that I needed three pages to explain it all. This is a rarity. In the case of action letters, you want people to know the pertinent facts.

When should you write action letters? Any time you want action. Usually this means you have a problem and you want it fixed. An added benefit of writing over speech is that when you write a letter, you can think it over. You can draft it and redraft it till it suits you. If the first draft is a little snotty, you can tone it down. You will not get nasty in your letter. You will be in control.

Let's say instead of writing a firm but polite letter to your landscaping service explaining the changes you need in your service, you call them on the phone. Maybe the person who answers the phone doesn't speak English well and doesn't understand what you want. By the time you get through to the owner, you are in such a huff you start out by yelling at him. So he might decide that you're just not worth the aggravation. Then you'll be stuck trying to find a new landscape service midsummer, and trust me, this will be no easy feat. A courteous but firm and direct letter is the way to go.

Finally, unlike a conversation, a letter is a document; it is a physical "thing" that exists. So in cases where letters go unheeded, and you end up making a claim or filing suit, you have proof of your efforts in what are now "official documents." This is why you should keep copies of action letters or other important letters you write. It's also why you should save all letters written to you.

For kicks, I am including some sample action letters, so you will understand the requisite tone—civil, direct, firm. I have changed the names and other incriminating information. You know why.

This one complains about the service at my local grocery store. It's clear why I was upset.

12 April 1998
Customer Relations
Gem Food Stores, Inc.
Melted Park, IL 6016X

Dear Sir or Madam:

Please address a situation I encountered at your store on Aspen Avenue in Darlington Heights, on Saturday, April 4, 1998. As I waited to check out (two customers were in front of me) a bagger named Harry G. was carrying on about how he should "paint my skin black or slant my eyes so that I will be eligible for food stamps." This is a direct quote. I could see that both customers in front of me were uncomfortable. The cashier, named Nanette, chimed in, "Yeah, they can't speak English, but they can figure out how to get food stamps." This is also a direct quote. Needless to say, all of us customers were incredulous.

This conversation between the employees—no customer joined in—continued past my turn to check out. I walked directly to the service desk and stood there with my mouth open until your employee asked what the problem was. I told her I was in shock, and then I asked her, "Why do you have racists working in your store?" I then quoted the conversation I had just heard, and she chortled and said, "Don't worry. I will talk to them."

I don't know if she ever talked to them. I still see all three of them in the store on a near-daily basis, and on a near-daily basis I am upset by that occurrence. I don't know why it has taken me a week to write to you. I really think I was in shock over it.

Of course, during the above offensive conversation, both employees were looking around to make sure no one might be overhearing to which their remarks apply. Well, I am not black, nor Asian, and I speak perfect English, but I could not have been more offended, and I would like to know what Gem's policy is regarding such conduct by its employees.

I look forward to a prompt response.

Very truly yours,
Margaret Basch

Both the regional manager and the store manager promptly called me to apologize and to tell me they do not tolerate racism among their employees. The store manager told me he took action against both employees, and I believe him. It's not really my business what action he took, but I felt better knowing that if nothing else the employees were told, "Don't do that again!"

It's also possible to write action letters by email, especially now that every business in America has a web site. It is even the preferred method to communicate by email when the transaction you wish to address occurred in cyberspace. Here is an example of a mild complaint letter I sent to my favorite on-line bookseller. They sell only used books, and I use it frequently to find rare books.

```
From LAWLADY@aol.com
To: Admin@bibliotomus.com
Hello. I use your service regularly. I
order books several times a week, on
average, and I like it very much, except
for one thing. About half the time that I
order a book I either get back an email
saying it is already sold or I never hear
```

```
from the bookseller (and don't get the
book). Would you PLEASE encourage your
booksellers to remove listings for books
that are sold? I don't mind spending
money for books I want but I do mind
wasting my time.
```

Even though this is a mild reproach, it is an action letter. I'm telling them what I want them to do and why I want them to do it. I don't say so directly, but they can guess that I won't continue to shop on their site if they continue to waste my time with outdated book offerings.

Give Good Response

A happy customer is a repeat customer and also a source of future referral business. What if you're on the receiving end of an action letter? What if *you* own a business and you get an angry missive about your service or product? Respond. Respond quickly and as positively as possible. If you really did screw up, acknowledge the mistake and make things right. If you investigate the complaint and you feel you are in the right, respond positively anyway. "We're sorry you were disappointed" might be appropriate. *Do not ignore an action letter.* Assume that someone who took the time to write you a letter has strong feelings. If the person threatens litigation, assume she will sue you. Decide what course of action you should take.

Keep an open mind. Maybe a particular employee *is* rude, or maybe a certain product is not up to your standards and should be discontinued. Maybe, just maybe, you can learn something by listening to a call for action from a client or customer.

On page 120 is the email response I got from the service

Subj: **RE: Sold books**
Date: 6/8/99 3:38:57 PM Central Daylight Time
From: admin@bibliotomus.com
To: LAWLADY@aol.com

Dear Law Lady,

I understand—and share!—your frustration!

Booksellers on Bibliotomus maintain their own records; we do
not add or delete their books.

We encourage booksellers to update their files often, and we
make it easy for them to do so (our on-line deletion entry
takes about a minute for an instant delete). There are,
however, great variations between booksellers in how often
they do update their files. Some dealers update them several
times a day, some once a day, once a week, once a month.
Beyond that, we insist that something be done or we close
that dealer's account (we have about 4000 members now, and
happily, we've only had to do that twice).

While there can be a 24-hour lag from the time a delete file
is imported to the time it disappears from the database, for
many subscribers, the problem is that the technology of the
Internet remains a bit daunting and intimidating, but I know
them to try hard to master it, and to service their customers
well. Bibliotomus members are a mixed bag in terms of style
and manner and the kind of books they enter, etc., but they
are generally a very good bunch of people. Thousands of
successful orders are sent out each day, and many booksellers
and bookbuyers write to tell us that not only have they made a
sale or found a book through this experience, but that they
have made many friends as well.

Our hope is that complaints TO THE BOOKSELLER from people
like you will encourage them to update their files on a more
timely basis. And you can also tell us who they are so that
we can bother them a bit.

And, of course, you are free to use the space on the order
form to ask the bookseller for confirmation that the book is,
indeed, available before you send any payment information.

I am sorry that this order did not work out for you, but hope
that in future, you will find in Bibliotomus only pleasure
and success!

Best wishes,

Van
Customer Service
Bibliotomus, Inc.

120

department of the on-line bookseller I wrote to. I'm including it because it shows that people and companies *do* respond to action letters. Bibliotomus could have ignored me or written back to say, "Tough luck, Margaret." Instead, they told me they feel my pain and they are doing everything in their power (meager as it may be) to fix my problem. So, I'm happy and I still use their service. If you want to maintain or grow a business, you will also have to respond positively to all feedback.

The Margaret Trick

I have a trick that works 90 percent of the time. I've never shared it with anyone before, and now I am sharing it with you. It is the Margaret Trick, and we shall keep it just among us girls.

Let's say you write an action letter for some service never rendered. You follow the form and you tell them what you want and what will happen if you don't get it (you'll sue them). They ignore you. This happens to me less frequently than it happens to other women, because I write my letters on my letterhead and so when I say I will sue, usually they believe me.

People don't always take threats of litigation seriously. Why should they? People say "I'll sue" all the time. And how many times have we heard "So sue me!" like it's a big joke? Is it any wonder the courts are all clogged up? The courts are full of lawsuits filed by fed-up people who want to be heard and want their complaints taken seriously. That is where the Margaret trick comes in.

This is how it works. You write a letter and you fax it to the party concerned. The letter says, "Attached hereto is a copy of the lawsuit which I am going to file on Monday (or two weeks from Friday) if you do not give me my money back (or fix my roof or take other appropriate action)." And of course, remember to attach a copy of the lawsuit.

So that's the trick. You write a letter, attach a copy of the law-suit, and explain why you are going to sue, and 90 percent of the time you will get your action or money without having to actually sue. Of course, 10 percent of the time you will have to follow through, but hey, ten beats a hundred.

Why does the Margaret Trick work? There's something about getting an official-looking piece of paper through the fax with a caption "In the Circuit Court of Cook County, Illinois" and the names of the parties on it that makes people want to take action. My sister recently combined the Margaret Trick with the "get the government to do your legal work for free" concept. She had taken her car to a local car dealer to have a leaky transmission fixed. Each time they charged her either four or six hundred dollars and each time they did not fix the leak. After the sixth visit, she asked for her money back for the unsuccessful repairs. They replied, "Oh, right, it probably needed that other thing, too."

First she talked, then she wrote a letter. Finally, sick of it, she faxed a letter to the manager of the dealership, with a copy of the Illinois Attorney General's consumer fraud complaint form. Here is her letter (which included a copy to the owner of dealership) and then the second, faxed, letter (with a copy to her lawyer sister). Again, names and locations are changed.

March 25, 1999
Mr. Jack Soloman
Trick Auto Dealer
5XX Small Drive
Schaumburg, IL 60173

Dear Mr. Soloman:

For approximately one year, I have been coming to the Trick Auto Shop in order to repair a transmission fluid leak in my Saab 900S. After spending $696.64, not counting tax, and many hours of my time, I still have the exact same transmission fluid leak as I did last year.

During my last repair stop at the Trick Auto Shop, I told the service advisor that if they did not fix the fluid leak that time, I would want my money back. And sure enough, the transmission fluid is still leaking. Enclosed are copies of the repair orders with the amount expended in parts and labor for the fluid leak. Please send a check for the total of $696.64 to:

Clara Basch
4XX Spring Street
Arlington Heights, IL 60005

If you have any questions, you may reach me at work at 312/814–3XXX.

Thank you for your prompt attention.

Sincerely,
Clara Basch

Enc.

This letter didn't have the desired effect. The next letter, a fax, was handwritten. It need not be fancy, as we have discussed:

April 13, 1999
Mr. Sullivan,

I have not received a response to my correspondence dated March 25, 1999 (see attachment 1). If I have not received a response in 5 business days, I will continue to the next step (see attachment 2).

Sincerely,
Clara Basch

cc: Margaret Basch
Attorney at Law

Guess what? Not only did they do the work again, they came to her house, picked up the car while she was at work, and delivered it after the work was completed. "Attachment 2" was the Illinois Attorney General's consumer fraud complaint. The dealer finally realized that it's better to fix a car than deal with a bureaucracy. Notice that even though the second letter was very short, it still told the recipient what action to take and what would happen if he did not take action.

Now, don't use the Margaret Trick willy-nilly. Don't threaten every little everybody with a lawsuit just because they don't suit you. You don't want to get a reputation as a whiner and a kvetch and a troublemaker. *Use it when you mean business*, and as a last resort, and then, if you still don't get action, follow through with your lawsuit (or in my sister's case, a consumer fraud complaint). *Otherwise you will become the girl who cried wolf and you will have even less power than you had before.*

Here is an example of one of the 10 percent of the cases in which the trick did not work for me, but I did follow through. I had a solicitation call from a prepaid legal plan that promised to refer business to me. They explained the whole plan on the phone and told me the cost was $700 per year, but because they were new and just setting up they would not charge my credit card until they sent me my first client.

Sure enough, they hung up the phone and charged me. I never heard from them again, and they would not give me back my seven hundred dollars. Now, maybe they figured I would not really sue them over seven hundred dollars. I still can't figure out why anyone would try to make a living scamming lawyers, but in any event, as a last resort to filing suit I faxed this letter and lawsuit:

Fax to LawScar

    In October of last year you charged my credit card $700 and I never heard from you again. I was told by Ms. Ashley

Regent that my card would not be charged until I received a referral from you. I have never received anything from you, and if you do not credit my card the $700 you obtained from me for bogus services within one week, I will file a civil suit and a complaint with the Illinois Attorney General.

Thank you for your attention.

Very truly yours,
Margaret M. Basch

They did not pay me and I did sue them. I took a huge default judgment against them, on which I will collect. This means they did not respond to the lawsuit, but since it did go to court, I "won" and the court awarded me a large sum of money that LawScar must legally pay.

Ack! I Can't Write a Letter!

Some people think they can't write a letter but almost everyone can. Some of us are afraid for any number of reasons. My mother, for example, is not a native English speaker. She speaks and reads English quite well, and she catches more typos than I do. I have her proofread for me for that reason. But she can't *write* in English without panicking over spelling and form. I understand this because I'm fluent in Spanish, but sometimes I can't figure out if something is two words or one. If you really don't have a grasp of the English language, get help. Just make sure the person helping you does have a command of written English, or the blind will be leading the blind, as they say.

If you think you can't write a letter because you have bad grammar or punctuation skills, write a draft and have someone who loves you fix it up. I dated a doctor with terrible language skills, and he writes laughable letters. I also worked for an attorney who could not write a cohesive sentence. He once wrote a five-page document with about thirty grammatical mistakes. It contained the sentence "The insurance company did it for its own self." What's that?

At any rate, if you send me a letter that I can't understand, I won't know your basics. If I'm a big corporation, I won't take action because either I will not understand what you want or I'll figure it out but will assume you are too dumb to actually do anything about it. After all, how smart can someone be if she can't write a short paragraph that makes sense?

I understand there are letter-writing services now that specialize in writing action letters for dissatisfied consumers. They charge a lot of money—in some cases more than a lawyer would charge to write the same letter. Do it yourself. If you need a little help from a friend, get it. There are also many books on letter writing. *Better Letters* by Jan Venolia, *How to Say It* by Rosalie Magglio, and *Just a Note to Say* by Florence Isaacs are three good ones. You can find them in the library in the 808 section.

These books have many samples in them so you can get some ideas if you really have fear of letter writing. They also have letters concerning congratulations and thanks. Obviously the forms in these books will not be the exact letters you need, but they will get you started.

Just Say Thanks

Say thank you as often as possible. Action letters and response letters are important, but no letter is more important than the thank you letter. Any time anybody does anything for you, send a thank you letter. What does it cost you? Thirty-three cents for a stamp, max. What does it gain you? A world of opportunities.

Let's say I do a good job for you on a case, and you spend your big settlement on a new house. Say one night, as you're sitting in front of your fireplace, you sit down and jot me a note:

Dear Margaret,
    Thank you for the hard work and special treatment you gave me during a very difficult time in my life.
                Sincerely,
                Karen

First off, I'll remember that letter forever because very few people send lawyers thank you notes. Second, I'll feel appreciated and I'll prize that feeling. So a year from now, when you need someone to make a phone call to the bank about a discrepancy with the mortgage, I am going to jump at the opportunity to do it for you. Because I know you'll appreciate it.

If your local grocer always goes out of his way to help you find things or determine prices, or if he is especially friendly, write to the owner or manager of the store and say how lucky they are to have this employee. Probably other people notice the young man's hard work and positive attitude, but you will most likely be the first to write a letter about it. What will it cost you? Thirty-three cents. What will you gain? The appreciation of the young man, and probably his boss, at being appreciated. And you'll be guaranteed good service at that grocery store for as long as you shop there.

I was at Marshall Field once, and I bought a little gift for a newborn baby. I can't remember what it was, but I remember the service I received. The clerk treated my purchase like it was the most important of her day, even though it was a small and inexpensive item. She boxed it and put lots of tissue in the box so that my item would look important to the recipient. She put a gift receipt in the box, and as she handed me my purchase, she asked if there was anything else she could do for me. People don't give service like that anymore, although we all wish they would. How can we encourage them to give us good service? Write a letter! If they don't think we care about good service, then why should they care about it? Since the clerk at Marshall Field was wearing a badge, I was able to make a mental note of her name. When I got home I wrote a letter to the baby department manager; I got her name by calling the store and asking for it. I told her what I just told you, and I'm quite sure that the clerk and her boss were thrilled—and I'm also sure the clerk was rewarded somehow for her professional courtesy.

To Whom Are You Speaking?

You know what you want to say—the product was wonderful; the service was slow. Whatever it was, it was important enough to YOU that you will take the time to write a letter. If it is important enough to write about, then it is important enough for you to want it read, and read by someone who will care enough to take action. If it is something that can be handled at a local level, then write locally. If a particular waiter was rude to you, for example, then write to the manager of that restaurant. If, however, the manager of the restaurant is rude to you, then you should write to a regional or national manager or director at the restaurant's headquarters. Sometimes you will need to work your way up. Let's say you buy a defective chain saw at a local branch of a national hardware store. You take it back to the store, and, of course, they tell you it's not their problem. You write to the manager of the store, and the manager blows you off, too. What do you do? If you can find a regional or national office, write there. Call information, look on the internet, or ask at the library for help. Try to get a name of a person, even if it's the president of the company; then write.

Every corporation that does business in your state must register with the Secretary of State. If you call the corporations department of your state's Secretary of State, they will have address information for every business that is incorporated and doing business in your state. If they are doing business but are not registered, call the attorney general in your state. If you exhaust your energy trying to get action from the people involved, don't forget, you've got the power of the government and the courts behind you.

Letters to the Editor

Who do you think has more power? Lawyers or journalists? It's probably a toss-up. If I find an unscrupulous business in town, I might be able to sue. A journalist can write about it, which could be worse. I have friends who are columnists. They are about as powerful as people can be. If a columnist in a widely read paper reports a scandal, everyone in town (or in the case of some papers, the country) will read about it. And columnists, because they are not just reporters but commentators, can put a "spin" on things. For example, when the syndicated columnist Bob Greene wrote about Canfield's Diet Fudge pop (he apparently liked it), grocery stores couldn't keep the stuff on the shelves for weeks after. Columnists have so much power that they have been known to get bogus convictions overturned and to have innocent men freed from death row.

How would you like to have that kind of power? You do. Well, sort of. If you write a good, clear, concise letter to your local paper, there is a good chance the paper will print it. Maybe you can right an injustice. You can shine a light on an important issue that the public might otherwise have missed. Chances are you will reach thousands if not millions of people by writing a good letter to an appropriate newspaper.

Why should a newspaper publish your letter? First of all, it's free. It fills space in the paper and they don't have to pay you for it. Second, newspapers, for all their freedom of the press, have self-imposed a duty of impartiality. If a columnist in your local paper writes a piece on a local controversy and you have a strong opinion on the same issue, write your side. Chances are the paper will publish your letter. Then you will have as much power as the regular newspaper columnist—at least on the day your letter is printed.

Sometimes you may simply want to bring an issue to the attention of your neighbors. Maybe you think the local library needs more books by women, but you can't convince the librarian. Write a persuasive letter to the editor. Get people to come around to your way of thinking. Others might then put some pressure on the librarian.

Here's a letter I wrote to my local paper when I spotted a private company selling cellular phones inside my local courthouse, just feet from the sheriff's post:

Kudos to Judge McBride

How peculiar that on the morning of Dec. 4 representatives of Hitel of Lincolnwood were selling cell phones and service inside the Rolling Meadows courthouse, at a table just feet from the sheriff's police charged with maintaining order in the place. When asked why cell phones were being sold inside the courthouse, the sheriff's police pleaded ignorance. Presiding Judge McBride, on the other hand, when asked why cell phones were being sold in the courthouse, flew through the courthouse in a rage and told the phone salesmen to "Pack it up! Right now!"

If the sheriff's police are selling, or better yet, giving away concessions in the courthouse, I would like to apply. A table advertising "Law Offices of Margaret M. Basch" inside the courthouse would be quite a coup. And I could save a fortune on office rent.

Kudos to Judge McBride for doing the right thing, and good luck to her in her position on the appellate court. Shame on the sheriff's police.

Margaret Basch
Schaumburg

I know that people read letters to the editor because every time I have one printed, I get calls from people—usually applauding my stand. In the case of this particular letter, others were outraged and glad to know that a private company was not allowed to sell product inside our taxpayer-supported courthouse. In any event, no one has sold anything at the courthouse since then.

You're Just a Girl

I'm going to tell you something now that should outrage you, but I hope it won't shock you. Some people are not going to take you seriously because you are a woman. This probably supports the trend toward unisex names for babies. No parent wants her child discriminated against. So we are finding fewer girls named Barbara and more named Montana.

When I was in law school, I worked in the legal department of a major corporation. Four of the attorneys there flew together on a trip from Chicago to Los Angeles. Something bad happened on the flight; I don't remember what it was, but it affected all four members of the party equally. All four of the attorneys wrote similar letters of complaint to the airline. Three of the attorneys got letters of apology from the airline along with a certificate for a free flight in the future. The fourth attorney got a letter of apology and an envelope. If you guessed that three of the attorneys were men, and one was a woman, you guessed right.

Of course, when the female attorney wrote to the airline again, this time sending copies of all four letters from the airline and pointing out the obvious sexism, the airline claimed "oversight." Of course we treat all our customers the same way, they urged. They did, in the end, send the fourth lawyer a free flight coupon.

In a case like that, proving sexism is easy. Usually, it's not. I can tell you that I have flown that airline and received horrible, outrageous "service," and when I complained about it (in a detailed three-page letter) they wrote back and said, "Well, hope you'll be happier with the service next time." Of course, there won't be a next time.

Remember that we're half the population, and more and more of us are gaining more and more power. We need to stand together and take a stand against bad service, inferior products, and second-rate politics. No business can afford to lose us *all*.

6

Practice Good Form

(HOW TO CHOOSE THE RIGHT FORMS AND USE THEM PROPERLY)

While I was writing this chapter I had lunch with another lawyer who was incensed when he learned I'd be telling women how to find and use forms. He acknowledged that he frequently produces documents by using forms, but he didn't think regular people should know it. A lot of lawyers probably feel the same way. But the fact is, no matter how much you pay a lawyer to generate a document, I can almost guarantee that he will have started with a form.

Some Basics

Earlier I wrote that the only useful task lawyers learn in law school is how to read cases. The most important skill lawyers learn after law school is how to create and use meaningful documents. Lawyers spend half their time speaking—in court, on the phone, in client interviews, and in depositions. The other half is spent writing—lawsuits, wills, contracts, briefs, orders, and memoranda.

When I first started practicing law, all the documents I used came out of a book. New lawyers are afraid to generate original papers. They think the legalese on forms is magical and makes their work seem professional and "lawyerly." In the dinosaur era, when I started out, legal documents were almost *required* to contain phrases like "the party of the first part" and "aforementioned" to be considered official. Thank goodness for the recent trend toward writing legal documents in (gasp!) plain English.

Which brings me to Margaret's Cardinal Rule of Forms: If you don't understand it, don't use it. I've come across many convoluted and jargon-crammed forms that even after several readings I still had no idea what the result of signing them would be. To make matters worse, forms directed at non-lawyers seem to have even more legal terminology than those intended for professionals. Maybe the publishers of these forms assume that eleven-dollar words and twenty-line sentences have intrinsic value. They don't. Words with more than thirteen letters are not the magic keys to legal locks.

Whether you're creating a document or using one produced by someone else, don't sign or ask anyone else to sign a document unless you grasp the consequences of doing so!

When you do understand a form and you're ready to sign it, do so on the lines provided for the signature. On documents longer than a page, it's also essential for every party to initial each page not requiring a signature. A prominent author I know entered into a multi-page limited partnership agreement. Years later his "partner" produced a document bearing the author's signature at the bottom. The body of the document stated, among other things, that for the rest of this author's life, he could only write for the limited partnership. The author swears he never signed such a document, yet his signature is at the end of the agreement. Whether the preceding pages were changed is a question that may never be answered without the intervention of a judge and jury. If the parties had initialed each page there would be no question as to their original contents.

Despite these cautions, forms are great tools. Women can accomplish many of their goals by using forms instead of, or in addition to, hiring a lawyer. Note well that while you can create all the documents you wish for yourself, you CANNOT write wills, leases, or other documents for your friends and neighbors. If you do, you'll be practicing law without a license, which is a big NO-NO!

Which Forms Can Be Used Without a Lawyer?

You name it: leases, contracts, notes, wills, liens, releases, mortgages, and lawsuits are just some of the documents you can successfully generate on your own. As long as you have the appropriate form, know what you want it to achieve, and are familiar with relevant laws as they apply to your situation, you can be your own lawyer with confidence.

Here's a quick review of common situations requiring forms:

- If you're having work done on your home, you'll want a contract with the various craftsmen and workers that will be involved in the project. It should detail costs and start and finish dates. You'll also need to understand how and why contractors and sub-contractors can put liens on your house.
- If you decide to represent yourself in court (it can and has been done), there are several documents you'll need to file with the court before trial date.
- If you sold something and the buyer took your item and then stopped payment on his check, there's a complaint form for small claims court you can fill out.

- If you rent property, you need a lease. However, in this instance I advise hiring a lawyer to prepare an initial lease. Go through each provision with her so you understand the language and what rights and obligations are being created for yourself and your tenant. When it comes time to create the next lease, either for the same property or another property, you can feel confident in creating it yourself.
- If you loan your best friend $500, you'll want to have her sign a promissory note.

Where Are the Forms?

Forms are readily available at stationery stores, in bookstores and libraries, on software programs, and even via the Internet. I'm not exaggerating when I say there are *millions* of forms available for free or for a small fee. All forms are intended to be copied and used at will and without obtaining "permission." That's why they're called forms.

Leases and rental agreements are often purchased at stationery stores. They can be purchased singly for less than one dollar, or you can purchase them on a disk for about five dollars. You can also copy one from a book at the library.

More than any other forms, do-it-yourself wills are generated from software programs. The problem with software is that you can't see the contents until after you buy it. So if you go this route, do some consumer research before you select a program. Will-writing software can be expensive compared to other sources of forms.

Cole Forms is one of my favorite sources of forms, but they are increasingly hard to find. Cole and every other form publisher has a list of available forms. If you see a list of forms, you might get ideas for using forms you hadn't thought of. One fairly good book of legal forms for consumers is Nolo Press's

101 Law Forms for Personal Use. Many of these 101 forms are worksheets and checklists. However, the book does contain many contracts, wills, and releases that are useful. It also comes with a computer disk, so you can view a form and read the instructions in the book, and then you can create the document on your computer and print it out. The book and disk cost about $25. Whether it's worth it to you depends on how many forms you think you can use. If you only need one or two, you might be better off finding them elsewhere or just copying them at the library. Nolo Press books are widely available at bookstores and libraries.

Professional form books for lawyers are excellent places to find good contracts. And as I mentioned at the beginning, the language in these documents is often easier to understand than in "consumer" books. They can be found at law libraries and bookstores.

Lawyer's reference books concerning specific topics also provide forms. These books are advantageous because along with getting the form, you can read about and understand the requirements under the laws of your state that the form pertains to. For example, a book on real estate law contains leases and purchase agreements. Many legal continuing education books also contain forms. For example, a legal continuing education book on mechanic's liens contains forms for liens. You will probably need to look for these in a law library because these books are intended for lawyers, but they are available to YOU.

Sample Forms

I've included some of the most requested and commonly used forms here for the purpose of showing what they look like and how they can be filled in to meet your needs. With the exception of the first living will form, don't use these forms. You'll need to do some homework to find just the right form to accomplish your goals.

Wills

When I first started practicing law, people asked me to draft their wills. My first reaction was, "I don't know how to draw up a will." The fact that I was a lawyer didn't automatically mean I knew how—they certainly didn't teach me in law school. But I did know about forms, and I picked clauses from several will forms to create my very first will. Now when someone wants a will, I use their individual information to create a new will, modifying previous wills with my current client's specifications.

How long does this take? Ten minutes, max. How long does it take other lawyers? About the same. How much do I charge for a simple will? I charge $50 for an individual will and $75 for a couple. How much do most other lawyers charge? Hundreds of dollars. But I'm not in the will business, so I only do them for existing clients. My point is, for the hundreds of dollars most lawyers will charge you, it pays to draft your own. You can spend the money you saved buying extra copies of this book for all your women friends!

Will Basics

We each have the inalienable right to express and carry out our last wishes, and a will is really the only way to accomplish this. So as you prepare to compose your will, think carefully about what you want to happen to your family and property when you die. Look at several different wills and compare their clauses. Find the ones that best suit your needs and put them together to make the one perfect will for you.

A will must be witnessed by two parties who won't benefit

from your death. Therefore, no one named in your will can be a witness. Strangers are your best bet. Each of you should sign or initial on each page of the will, and sign it at the end.

The executor should be someone who has agreed *in advance* to take the job. When you die, the executor you name in your will will have a big responsibility in carrying out your wishes and answering to the probate court. You'll also need to name an alternate executor (in case the executor becomes unavailable or dies, or decides he no longer wants the responsibility of handling your estate).

You need to decide what you want to happen to your estate. There are no rules here. It is your WILL. You can specify any kind of bequests (gifts) you wish in *your will*. If you want your body cremated or donated to science, put it in your will. If you intend to leave Aunt Edna's priceless gold earrings to *me*, or to your sister, put it in your will. Funeral arrangements are also often stipulated in wills. Most people include the provision that funeral expenses will be paid by the estate.

As you may have guessed, the smaller your estate, the less likely it is you need a lawyer or an estate plan. Most people, married or single, who have limited assets—a home, some personal possessions, and a medium-sized bank account—only need a simple will. If you own several homes or have hundreds of thousands of dollars in investments, or if you want to create a special trust for charitable purposes, or otherwise do something out of the ordinary, then you may need to consult a lawyer. You will want to consider tax implications.

Spouse, Partners, and Children

Most married people leave everything to their spouse, and to their children if their spouse predeceases them (dies first). If you're not married, but have a life partner or special friends, they need to be specifically named in a will if you want them to inherit all or part of your estate. The law makes no automatic provisions for people other than family members.

You can't "disinherit" your spouse because he has a marital interest in your estate. You can disown your adult children but you can't disown children who are considered minors or dependents. If you have minor children, you should specify in your will who should have custody of your children if you and the children's father both die. You should also specify who should control the money you leave to any minor children in your will.

If you leave a portion of your estate to your daughters Daisy and Dotty, and Daisy, God forbid, dies before you, then you need to decide what should happen to Daisy's share. Should it go to Daisy's husband and children? Or should her share go to Dotty? Keep in mind that your will is not carved in stone. It is legally binding, but it is only a piece of paper, and it can be torn to smithereens and rewritten. A new will supersedes a previous one, so you can always change your mind. If Daisy dies before you and your will says her share will pass to her husband, and then her husband remarries and you decide you don't want him to share in your estate, you can change your will.

Ensuring the Safety of Your Will

Finally, keep your original will where you keep your important papers, like your safe deposit box. Make sure the executor knows where to find this original. Keep an *unsigned* copy at home for periodic updating. *Never make copies of your signed will,* because a signed copy can look like an original. The father of someone I knew made a will as he lay dying in the hospital. After the man's death, his wife probated an earlier will. What happened to the later will is open to conjecture. If he had destroyed the first will and left no copies, then that will could not have been probated. So his final wishes were not fulfilled. It's sad, but it is also the reason that wills have so many rules attached to them.

Sample Wills

On pages 142–144 is a basic will that I prepared for a client several years ago. He left everything to his wife and then to his children in the event that his wife predeceased him. You'll notice that the children are not named in the will. The spouse is named, the alternate executor is named, and the children's guardian is named. At the time this will was drawn, the man had three children. However, what if after the will was signed the couple had a fourth child? Leaving estates to "my children who survive me" includes existing children and later-born children.

On pages 145–146 is a will I copied from a book at the library. *American Jurisprudence Legal Forms, Second Edition* is a multiple-volume set that has as many forms as you can think of and some you never would have thought of. It is published by Lawyers Cooperative Publishing and lawyers use these books frequently. It includes many wills. If the gentleman above had used this form, the results would be quite different.

LAST WILL AND TESTAMENT OF
PAUL D. FRANKLIN

I, PAUL D. FRANKLIN, a resident of Illinois, declare
this to be my Will, and I revoke all other wills and codicils
that I have made.

SECTION I

I name my wife, Marilyn Franklin, as executor of this
Will. If for any reason my wife fails or ceases to act as executor, then I name my brother, David Franklin, as executor of
this Will. I direct that no security on the executor's
bond be required.

1. I direct the executor to pay out of my estate passing hereunder, after satisfaction of the gift or gifts made
herein, all expenses of administering my estate, inheritance, transfer and succession taxes (including interest and
penalties, if any) which become due by reason of my death. I
waive on behalf of my estate any right to
recover from any person, including any beneficiary of
insurance upon my life, any part of such taxes.

2. I give the executor the following powers and
discretions, in each case to be exercisable without
court order:

a) To sell at public or private sale, to retain, to
   lease, to borrow money and for that purpose to
   mortgage or to pledge, all or part of the real or
   personal property of my estate;
b) To settle claims in favor of or against my
   estate;
c) To exercise or not to exercise any election or
   option granted to executors by the Internal
   Revenue Code in force at my death, even though
   such exercise or non-exercise increases or
   decreases estate principal or income, without
   adjustment to principal or income.
d) To distribute the residue of my estate in case or
   in kind or partly in each, and for this
   purpose the determination of the executor as to
   the value of any property distributed in kind
   shall be conclusive; and
e) To execute and deliver any deeds, contracts,
   mortgages, bills of sale or other instruments
   necessary or desirable for exercise of his or her
   powers and discretions as executor.

SECTION II

No person named in this Will shall be deemed to have survived me unless he or she is living on the thirtieth day succeeding the day of my death.

SECTION III

I devise and bequeath all my property, real, personal and mixed, to my wife, Marilyn Franklin, if she survives me, otherwise to my children who survive me, in equal shares.

SECTION IV

I give the residue of my estate to my wife, if she survives me; otherwise, I leave the residue of my estate to my children who survive me, in equal shares.

SECTION V

1. The expenses of my last illness, my funeral and the administration of my estate, wherever situated, shall be paid out of the principal of my residuary estate.

2. All inheritance, estate and succession taxes, including interest and penalties, payable by reason of my death shall be paid out of and be charged generally against the principal of my residuary estate without reimbursement from any person, except that my executor shall have the right to claim reimbursement for any such taxes which become payable on account of property over which I have a power of appointment.

SECTION VI

If my wife does not survive me I appoint my brother-in-law, Mark Carter, as guardian of any of my children who are still less than eighteen years old on the date of my death. I direct that no guardian's bond be required of any guardian named herein. If any beneficiary under this Article is a minor at the time of distribution, my Executor may distribute his share to the guardian herein named. The receipt of same by such guardian shall be a sufficient discharge to my Executor.

Such guardian may hold such property for, or
distribute it to, the beneficiary, or sell it and hold and
invest the proceeds or expend them for the beneficiary. When
the beneficiary reaches majority, any undistributed property or
proceeds thereof shall be delivered to the beneficiary.
If the beneficiary dies before reaching majority, any
undistributed property or proceeds thereof shall be
distributed as if they were part of his or her estate.

I have signed this Will, constituting three (3)
typewritten pages, this page included, and have initialed the
preceding page on _____.
                                    (date)

_____(seal)

We certify that the above-named Testator signed the foregoing instrument and acknowledged it to be his Will. In the
presence of Testator and in the presence of each other we sign
our names below as witnesses. We believe Testator to be of
sound mind and memory.

_____ residing at _____

_____ residing at _____

Subscribed and sworn to before me this 15th
day of September, 1992.

_____

This document prepared by Margaret M. Basch, P.O. Box
805, Mount Prospect, IL 60056.

§ 266:78 Married person's will—Estate to spouse—Short form

Will of ____1____

I, ____2____ *[name of testator],* ____3____ *[if appropriate, add:* also known as ____4____ and ____5____ *or if wife's will add:* formerly known as ____6____ *(maiden name),]* of ____7____ *[address],* ____8____ County, ____9____ *[state],* declare this to be my last will and testament.

I.

I revoke all previous wills and codicils.

II.

1. I am married and the name of my ____10____ *[wife or* husband] is ____11____.

2. All references in this will to my ____12____ *[wife or* husband] are to ____13____ *[name].*

III.

If no children:
I have no children, living or dead.

If children:
1. I have ____14____ *[number]* living children, issue of my marriage to ____15____, as follows: ____16____ *[such as:* ____17____, *a boy, born on* ____18____ *(date),* and ____19____, *a girl, born on* ____20____ *(date)].*

2. I have ____21____ *[number]* living children, issue of a previous marriage to ____22____ *[former spouse],* as follows: ____23____ *[insert names and birth dates of children].*

3. I have a deceased child, ____24____ *[name],* who died on ____25____ *[date],* and who leaves surviving ____26____ *[insert names and addresses of descendants].*

4. References in this will to my ____27____ *[child or* children] include any of my children that may hereafter be born or adopted.

IV.

I have, except as otherwise provided in this will, intentionally and with full knowledge, omitted to provide for my heirs who may be living at the time of my death, including any person or persons who may, after the date of this will, become my heir or heirs by reason of marriage or otherwise.

V.

1. I give all of my property, real, personal, and mixed ____28____ [excluding my ____29____ (husband's *or* wife's) share of our community property,] to my ____30____ [wife *or* husband], provided ____31____ [she *or* he] survives me ____32____ *[if desired, add:* for ____33____ days].

2. If ____34____ [he *or* she] does not so survive me, then I give my estate to my ____35____ [children *or* issue] who survive me ____36____ *[if desired, add:* for ____37____ days], per stirpes.

VI.

1. I nominate and appoint ____38____ *[name]* as the executor of this will, to serve ____39____ [with *or* without] bond.

2. If ____40____ [she *or* he] should predecease me, or for any reason fails to qualify or declines to act as executor, I nominate and appoint ____41____ *[name of individual or corporate executor]* of ____42____ *[address],* ____43____ County, ____44____ *[state],* as executor of this will to serve ____45____ [with *or* without] bond.

I subscribe my name to this will on ____46____ *[date],* at ____47____ *[address],* ____48____ County, *[state],* in the presence of ____49____, ____50____, and ____51____, attesting witnesses, who subscribe their names to this will on ____52____ *[date]* at my request and in my presence.

[Signature]

ATTESTATION CLAUSE

On the date last above written, ____53____ *[testator's name],* known to us to be the person whose signature appears at the end of this will, declared to us, the undersigned, that the foregoing instrument, consisting of ____54____ pages, including the page on which we have signed as witnesses, was ____55____ [his *or* her] will. ____56____ [He *or* She] then signed the will in our presence, and at ____57____ [his *or* her] request, in____ 58____ [his *or* her] presence and in the presence of each other, we now sign our names as witnesses.

____59____, *[Signature]*	residing at	____60____ *[Street, city, state]*
____61____, *[Signature]*	*residing at*	____62____ *[Street, city, state]*
____63____, *[Signature]*	*residing at*	____64____ *[Street, city, state]*

Finally, as a test, I had my brother create a will with some direction from me. He owns one of the popular software programs for will writing. You can compare it to the will that I prepared for the same people above. Despite its minor variations, its effect is the same as the first sample.

Will of Paul D. Franklin

I, Paul D. Franklin, a resident of Illinois, Cook County, declare that this is my will. My Social Security Number is 123-45-6789.

FIRST: I revoke all wills and codicils that I have previously made.

SECOND: I am married to Marilyn Franklin.

THIRD: I have the following children now living: Alice Franklin, Betty Franklin, and Cindy Franklin.

FOURTH: As used in this will, the term "specific bequest" refers to all specifically identified property, both real and personal, that I give to one or more beneficiaries in this will. The term "residuary estate" refers to the rest of my property not otherwise specifically disposed of by this will or in any other manner. The term "residuary bequest" refers to my residuary estate that I give to one or more beneficiaries in this will.

FIFTH: All personal property I give in this will through a specific or residuary bequest is given subject to any purchase-money security interest, and all real property I give in this will through a specific or residuary bequest is given subject to any deed of trust, mortgage, lien, assessment, or real property tax owed on the property. As used in this will, "purchase-money security interest" means any debt secured by collateral that was incurred for the purpose of purchasing that collateral. As used in this will, "non-purchase-money security interest" means any debt that is secured by collateral but which was not incurred for the purpose of purchasing that collateral.

SIXTH: When this will states that a beneficiary must survive me for the purpose of receiving a specific bequest or residuary bequest, he or she must survive me by 45 days, except that property left to my spouse shall pass free of this 45-day survivorship requirement.

SEVENTH: I hereby leave $1.00 to each of the following persons: Alice Franklin, Betty Franklin, and Cindy Franklin. These bequests are in addition to and not instead of any other specific bequest that this will makes to these persons.

EIGHTH: I give my residuary estate to my wife, Marilyn Franklin. However, if the beneficiary named in this paragraph to receive my residuary estate fails to survive me, that beneficiary's living children shall take the residuary estate.

NINTH: Any specific bequest or residuary bequest made in this will to two or more beneficiaries shall be shared equally among them, unless unequal shares are specifically indicated.

TENTH: If my spouse and I should die simultaneously, or under such circumstances as to render it difficult or impossible to determine who predeceased the other, I shall be conclusively presumed to have survived my spouse for purposes of this will.

ELEVENTH: If at my death there is no living person who is entitled by law to the custody of my minor child or children and who is available to assume such custody, I name Mark Carter, Marilyn's brother, as guardian of my minor child or children, to serve without bond. If this person shall for any reason fail to qualify or cease to act as guardian, I name Susan Carter, Marilyn's sister, as guardian instead, also to serve without bond.

TWELFTH: All specific bequests and residuary bequests made in this will to Alice Franklin, Betty Franklin, and Cindy Franklin shall be given to Mark Carter, Marilyn's brother, as custodian for Alice Franklin, Betty Franklin, and Cindy Franklin under the Illinois Uniform Transfers to Minors Act. If Mark Carter, Marilyn's brother, cannot serve as custodian of property left to Alice Franklin, Betty Franklin, and Cindy Franklin under this will, Susan Carter, Marilyn's sister, shall serve instead.

THIRTEENTH: I wish to forgive the following debt(s) plus accrued interest as of the date of my death: David Franklin, 1/1/99, $2,000.

FOURTEENTH: I name my wife, Marilyn Franklin, as my personal representative (executor), to serve without bond. If this person or institution shall for any reason fail to qualify or cease to act as personal representative, I name my brother, David Franklin, as personal representative (also to serve without bond), instead.

FIFTEENTH: I direct my personal representative to take all actions legally permissible to have the probate of my will done as simply and as free of court supervision as possible under the laws of the state having jurisdiction over this will, including filing a petition in the appropriate court for the independent administration of my estate.

SIXTEENTH: I hereby grant to my personal representative the following powers, to be exercised as he or she deems to be in the best interests of my estate:

1) To retain property without liability for loss or depreciation resulting from such retention.

2) To dispose of property by public or private sale, or exchange, or otherwise, and

receive and administer the proceeds as a part of my estate.

3) To vote stock, to exercise any option or privilege to convert bonds, notes, stocks or other securities belonging to my estate into other bonds, notes, stocks or other securities, and to exercise all other rights and privileges of a person owning similar property.

4) To lease any real property that may at any time form part of my estate.

5) To abandon, adjust, arbitrate, compromise, sue on or defend and otherwise deal with and settle claims in favor of or against my estate.

6) To continue or participate in any business which is a part of my estate, and to effect incorporation, dissolution or other change in the form of organization of the business.

7) To do all other acts which in his or her judgment may be necessary or appropriate for the proper and advantageous management, investment and distribution of my estate.

The foregoing powers, authority and discretion granted to my personal representative are intended to be in addition to the powers, authority and discretion vested in him or her by operation of law by virtue of his or her office, and may be exercised as often as is deemed necessary or advisable, without application to or approval by any court in any jurisdiction.

SEVENTEENTH: Except for purchase-money security interests on personal property passed in this will, and deeds of trust, mortgages, liens, taxes and assessments on real property passed in this will, I instruct my personal representative to pay all debts and expenses, including non-purchase-money secured debts on personal property, owed by my estate using my residuary estate.

EIGHTEENTH: I instruct my personal representative to pay all estate and inheritance taxes assessed against property in my estate or against my beneficiaries out of all the property in my taxable estate, on a pro-rata basis.

NINETEENTH: If any beneficiary under this will in any manner, directly or indirectly, contests or attacks this will or any of its provisions, any share or interest in my estate given to the contesting beneficiary under this will is revoked and shall be disposed of in the same manner as if that contesting beneficiary had failed to survive me and left no living children.

I, Paul D. Franklin, the testator, sign my name to this instrument, this _____ day of _____, ____. I hereby declare that I sign and execute this instrument as my last will, that I sign it willingly, and that I execute it as my free and voluntary act for the purposes therein expressed. I declare that I am of the age of majority or otherwise legally empowered to make a will, and under no constraint or undue influence.

_____

(Signed)

We, the witnesses, sign our names to this instrument, and do hereby declare that the testator willingly signed and executed this instrument as the testator's last will.

Each of us, in the presence of the testator, and in the presence of each other, hereby signs this will as witness to the testator's signing.

To the best of our knowledge, the testator is of the age of majority or otherwise legally empowered to make a will, is mentally competent, and under no constraint or undue influence.

We declare under penalty of perjury, that the foregoing is true and correct, this _____ day of _____, _____.

Witness #1: _____

Residing at: _____

Witness #2: _____

Residing at: _____

Witness #3: _____

Residing at: _____

****

AFFIDAVIT

STATE OF _____, COUNTY OF _____

I, the undersigned, an officer authorized to administer oaths, certify that _____, the testator, and _____, _____, and _____, the witnesses, whose names are signed to the attached or foregoing instrument and whose signatures appear below, having appeared together before me and having been first duly sworn, each then declared to me that:

1) the attached or foregoing instrument is the last will of the testator;

2) the testator willingly and voluntarily declared, signed and executed the will in the presence of the witnesses;

3) the witnesses signed the will upon request by the testator, in the presence and hearing of the testator, and in the presence of each other;

4) to the best knowledge of each witness the testator was, at that time of the signing, of the age of majority (or otherwise legally competent to make a will), of sound mind, and under no constraint or undue influence; and

5) each witness was and is competent, and was then 18 years of age or older.

Testator: _____ Witness: _____

Witness: _____ Witness: _____

Subscribed, sworn to and acknowledged before me by _____, the testator, and by _____, _____, and _____, witnesses, this _____ day of _____, ____.

SIGNED: _____

Living Wills

A living will prevents medical care providers from using extraordinary means to keep individuals alive. You don't need a living will if you want to be kept alive at all costs. Otherwise, get a form.

There's absolutely no reason to engage a lawyer to draft a living will. All you need to do is sign a form in front of two witnesses and then have the witnesses sign it. The witnesses should not be your family members, beneficiaries, or doctors because they might be deemed to have a conflict. Again, strangers make the best witnesses. Make sure you give the original to a person who will be responsible for making decisions about your medical care—an "attorney in fact"—such as a husband, parent, child, or friend, if you are unable to speak your desires. For understandable reasons, doctors and hospitals are reluctant to withhold medical care under any circumstances. But a living will changes the playing field.

The first form below is the basic Living Will form that I use, and you can feel free to use it, too.

LIVING WILL DECLARATION

I,_____ , being of sound mind,
willfully and voluntarily make known my desires that my
moment of death shall not be artificially postponed.

If at any time I have an incurable and irreversible
injury, disease, or illness judged to be a terminal condition
by my attending physician who has personally examined me and
has determined that my death is imminent except for death
delaying procedures, I direct that such procedures which would
only prolong the dying process be withheld or withdrawn, and
that I be permitted to die naturally with only the
administration of medication, sustenance, or the performance
of any medical procedure deemed necessary by attending
physician to provide me with comfort care.

In the absence of my ability to give directions
regarding the use of such death delaying procedures, it is my
intention that this Declaration shall be honored by my family
and physician as the final expression of my legal right to
refuse medical or surgical treatment and accept the
consequences from such refusal.

Date _____   X _____
                                    Declarant

Witness: _____
                name and address

Witness: _____
                name and address

In Illinois we have a statute called the "Illinois Living Will Act," 755 ILCS 35, *et seq*. It uses a different form from the Living Will Declaration on the previous page, but specifies "the declaration may, but need not, be in the following form, and in addition may include other specific directions."

Illinois Living Will

DECLARATION

This Declaration is made this ____ day of _____ (month) , _____ (year). I, _____ (name), being of sound mind, willfully and voluntarily make known my desires that my moment of death shall not be artificially postponed.

If at any time I should have an incurable and irreversible injury, disease, or illness judged to be a terminal condition by my attending physician who has personally examined me and has determined that my death is imminent except for death delaying procedures, I direct that such procedures which will only prolong the dying process be withheld or withdrawn, and that I be permitted to die naturally with only the administration of medication, sustenance, or the performance of any medical procedure deemed necessary by my attending physician with comfort care.

In the absence of my ability to give directions regarding the use of such death delaying procedures, it is my intention that this Declaration should be honored by my family and physician as the final expression of my legal right to refuse medical or surgical treatment and accept the consequences from such refusal.

Signed _____

City, County and State of Residence:_____

The Declarant is personally known to me and I believe him or her to be of sound mind. I saw the Declarant sign the Declaration in my presence (or the Declarant acknowledged in my presence that he or she signed the Declaration) and I sign the Declaration as a witness in the presence of the Declarant. I did not sign the Declarant's signature above for or at the direction of the Declarant. At the date of this instrument, I am not entitled to any portion of the estate of the Declarant according to the laws of intestate succession or, to the best of my knowledge and belief under any will of Declarant or other instrument taking effect at Declarant's death, or directly financially responsible for Declarant's medical care.

Witness: _____

Witness: _____

The next living will is from *Legal-Wise* by Carl W. Battle. It's a good example of a living will form that can be copied from a book at the library. It's also different from the other two forms in that it provides for a durable power of attorney. It names a person who will be responsible for making your medical decisions if you become unable to make or express your own decisions.

Living Will

1. I,_____(Maker), being of sound mind voluntarily declare that this directive is made this _____ day of _____, 19___ as my Living Will in accordance with the laws of the State of _____.

2. If I should have at any time an incurable condition caused by illness, disease, or injury certified to be a terminal condition by two licensed physicians, and where there is no reasonable expectation of recovery from said terminal condition, and where the application of life-sustaining methods and equipment would only prolong the moment of my imminent death, I hereby direct and request that said life-sustaining methods and equipment not be used, and that I be allowed to die naturally and not be kept alive by artificial or extraordinary means.

3. In the event that I am unable to give conscious direction regarding medical treatment or the use of said life-sustaining procedures, I direct and request that this Living Will be honored by my family, physicians and all others as the final and conclusive expression of my legal right to refuse medical treatment. I hereby appoint _____ as my true and lawful attorney in fact to act for me and make decisions concerning medical treatment, including the withdrawal or withholding of life support, in accordance with this Living Will. This power of attorney shall remain in effect in the event that I should become or be declared disabled, incapacitated, or incompetent.

4. This Living Will shall be in effect until it is revoked by me.

5. My current residence is: _____

In Witness Whereof I have signed this document as my declaration and Living Will.

_____   _____
          Maker's Signature   Date

The maker of this Living Will is personally known to me, is of sound mind, and has executed this document of his or her own free will.

_____   _____
          Witness' Signature   Address

_____   _____
          Witness' Signature   Address

_____   _____
          Witness' Signature   Address

Subscribed and sworn to before me on this _____ day of _____, 19___.

_____
                    Notary

Promissory Notes

If you're lending money, you need a promissory note. The important items to include in it are the names of the lender and the borrower and the terms of repayment, including the *due date*. If there will be interest owed on the loan, this amount or rate should also be spelled out. The following is a form available at a big office supply chain. The producer of the form is E-Z Legal Forms.

The basic terms of the loan are pretty easy to fill out on this form. The first three paragraphs are standard, although they could be expressed more simply. First, if a partial payment is made, it will be applied first to interest and then to the balance of the loan. Second, if the borrower is late with payment, the lender will consider the entire amount due (this is so you can sue for entire balance immediately instead of waiting for the end of the payment plan). Third, if the borrower defaults, he may be held responsible for the lender's attorney's fees and also penalties. Those things I understand.

Now look at that big, ugly paragraph in the middle of this promissory note. Every time I look at it my eyes glaze over, so don't stare at it too long or I might lose you. The first sentence of that big fat paragraph is four and two-thirds lines long! I don't know what it says, and the paragraph goes downhill from there. This form, for me, violates Margaret's Cardinal Rule of Forms. I don't understand it, so I won't use it. If *you* understand it, feel free.

Actually, I do understand it, but I had to read that first sesquipedalian sentence a half dozen times before it sunk in. Overcoming the eye-glaze factor makes this form not worth using for me. There are simpler promissory notes that will accomplish the same thing. Again, read through several forms and decide on the best one for you. If you like different parts of different forms, you can cut and paste.

PROMISSORY NOTE

A293-10
R293-04
BB240

$

Principal Amount

Dated:

State of

(year)

FOR VALUE RECEIVED, the undersigned hereby jointly and severally promise to pay to the order of

, the sum of

Dollars ($), together with interest thereon at the rate of   % per annum on the unpaid balance. Said sum shall be paid in the manner following:

All payments shall be first applied to interest and the balance to principal. This note may be prepaid, at any time, in whole or in part, without penalty. All prepayments shall be applied in reverse order of maturity.

This note shall at the option of any holder hereof be immediately due and payable upon the failure to make any payment due hereunder within   days of its due date.

In the event this note shall be in default, and placed with an attorney for collection, then the undersigned agree to pay all reasonable attorney fees and costs of collection. Payments not made within five (5) days of due date shall be subject to a late charge of   % of said payment. All payments hereunder shall be made to such address as may from time to time be designated by any holder hereof.

The undersigned and all other parties to this note, whether as endorsers, guarantors or sureties, agree to remain fully bound hereunder until this note shall be fully paid and waive demand, presentment and protest and all notices thereto and further agree to remain bound, notwithstanding any extension, renewal, modification, waiver, or other indulgence by any holder or upon the discharge or release of any obligor hereunder or to this note, or upon the exchange, substitution, or release of any collateral granted as security for this note. No modification or indulgence by any holder hereof shall be binding unless in writing; and any indulgence on any one occasion shall not be an indulgence for any other or future occasion. Any modification or change of terms, hereunder granted by any holder hereof, shall be valid and binding upon each of the undersigned, notwithstanding the acknowledgment of any of the undersigned, and each of the undersigned does hereby irrevocably grant to each of the others a power of attorney to enter into any such modification on their behalf. The rights of any holder hereof shall be cumulative and not necessarily successive. This note shall take effect as a sealed instrument and shall be construed, governed and enforced in accordance with the laws of the State first appearing at the head of this note. The undersigned hereby execute this note as principals and not as sureties.

Signed in the presence of:

Witness _____   Borrower _____

Witness _____   Borrower _____

GUARANTY

We the undersigned jointly and severally guaranty the prompt and punctual payment of all moneys due under the aforesaid note and agree to remain bound until fully paid. In the presence of:

Witness _____   Guarantor _____

Witness _____   Guarantor _____

I know someone who lent money he could not afford to lose—which is another of my cardinal rules that I don't need to explain. He thought he was doing everything right by having the borrower sign a promissory note. The form he chose was pretty basic, however, and he tried to fancy it up with some legalese of his own. When the borrower stopped taking my friend's calls, my friend forwarded the promissory note to me.

He put the following payment information on the note: if the borrower paid by August 1, she wouldn't owe interest, but if she paid after August 1, she'd owe one percent interest per month. I must have read that promissory note four times. When was the money due and when was the borrower in default? There is that August 1 date, but if the money is due on that date, then why is there interest on the loan amount after that date? The one percent was stated as interest and not as a late fee, so I was distressed. I called another lawyer who was equally amazed and then said, "It must be a demand note. If there is no due date then the loan is due when the lender demands repayment." I figured that if we sued the woman she would not bother hiring a lawyer or appearing in court. If she could afford to defend the case, she could afford to pay the loan, after all. We were not talking about a lot of money, just more than my friend could afford to lose. The moral of the story is, look at several forms. The things they have in common are probably important. In a promissory note, the due date is one of them.

Here is the simplest type of promissory note (the kind I would use if I were generous enough to lend money):

$500.00 Schaumburg, Illinois, May 1, 2000
   I hereby acknowledge receipt of the sum Five Hundred Dollars from Margaret Basch and agree to repay the said sum at the rate of Fifty Dollars per week for ten weeks, with the first payment due on May 29, 2000. X_____

You could have such a note witnessed. You could add a clause for interest and one for penalties. You can include a provision for attorneys' fees. You might want to think about including a clause that if you grant an extension of time for payment that you are not waiving your right to enforce the note. Again, you can use a form for these provisions or you can just write what you are comfortable with.

More Everyday Legal Forms by Irving J. Sloan includes three attorney's fee provisions and three for extension of time. Here is one sample of each type:

Fee Provision:
The makers and indorsers hereof agree to pay all costs of collection, whether payment hereof be enforced by suit or otherwise, and costs to include a reasonable attorney's fee.

Extension:
The makers and indorsers severally waive any defense which they might have on account of any extension or extensions of time that may be granted to any one or more of them.

If you understand these clauses and they say what you want to say in your promissory note, then by all means, throw them in.

In Chapter Seven I will tell you how you can represent yourself in court. Some of the forms you will need to do that will be available from the clerk of the court (i.e., a summons). There are also forms for Complaints, Answers, Interrogatories, and everything else you may need to file, but they're not available from the clerk's office. You can find these forms in reference books. You can buy legal how-to books on representing yourself that have forms, and there are books we lawyers use. Either will work fine, but you will probably find a wider variety of forms in lawyers' books because a legal how-to book cannot cover every possible situation under which you might want to sue. In legal form books you can find Complaints (and Answers and Interrogatories) for car accidents, slip and falls, property damage, defamation, you name it. By the way, when you hear that someone filed a lawsuit, what was filed was really a Complaint. This is also called "Complaint at Law." Filing a Complaint with the clerk of court starts the legal process. When served on a Defendant with a summons it requires his attendance in court. The process is the same in Federal and in State court.

Here is a form from West's Illinois Forms for a stop-ordered check. You would use this form if someone paid you by check and then stopped payment. Say, for example, you sold a piece of furniture through an ad in the paper and the buyer took your furniture and then stopped payment on the check. If the amount of the sale is small you might not want to hire an attorney to collect the amount for you, but you also might not want to let it go. Going to small claims court and using a form Complaint like this one is a good alternative. As you can see, it is pretty simple to fill out.

COMPLAINT

Plaintiff, _____, by_____ [AB, his; CD, her] attorney, complaining of Defendant, _____ [drawer], alleges:

1. On _____ [date], at _____, Illinois, for value received, Defendant made and delivered to Plaintiff Defendant's check for $_____ [amount], a copy whereof is hereto attached as part hereof, marked "Exhibit A."

2. On _____ [date], at _____, Illinois, said check was duly endorsed and presented to the drawee, _____ [Bank], which thereupon refused to pay same, Defendant having directed it, by written stop-payment order, not to pay the same.

3. Plaintiff is the owner and holder of said check, on which there remains due and owing by Defendant to Plaintiff, the sum of $_____, with interest thereon from _____ [date].

WHEREFORE Plaintiff requests judgment against Defendant for the sum of $_____, with interest from _____ [*date*], plus costs of suit herein.

_____
_____, Attorney for Plaintiff

_____ [Attorney (& Firm)]
Attorney No.: _____
_____ [Phone]
_____ [Address]

A caption on a lawsuit is the name of the case. When you get a blank Complaint form from the clerk of your court it will give the name of the court: "In the Circuit Court of Cook County, Illinois, Municipal Department, Third District." You will add your name as Plaintiff and the Defendant's name: "Margaret Basch, Plaintiff, vs. Tom Jones, Defendant," and then the clerk will assign you a case number. Those things are the caption. They will first appear on the Complaint (also called the lawsuit) and then on every other document filed in the case, including the summons, answer, and any motions, orders, and discovery documents.

So the next time you think about calling your lawyer, or worry whether you should let a problem go because "it's not worth hiring a lawyer for," consider whether you might be able to solve the problem with a form. Forms can simplify your life, enforce your rights under the law, and create records of your intent. So use forms and be empowered!

7

When to Hire a Lawyer (and When to Fire One), and When to Do It Yourself

This book cannot make you a lawyer, but it can empower you by giving you certain tools. Sometimes you will be able to use these tools to avoid hiring a lawyer. You will be able to look up the answer to a legal question. You will be able to generate some documents. You might be able to avoid litigation to resolve a problem by writing a firm letter. However, there will be times when you will WANT the help of a lawyer. It will be up to you. With the right tools and a little background you will be able to make the best decision.

What to Expect from a Lawyer-Client Relationship

I am the world's greatest lawyer. Unfortunately, I can't represent you all. So, how to find the best lawyer for you? One with whom you can have a happy and productive relationship, based on mutual respect? Hmmm. Sounds like hiring a lawyer is like finding a mate. Well, I love my clients and my clients love me. I am not saying that you should love your lawyer, although it is nice when you do. At the very least, you need to be able to trust and respect your lawyer. At the same time, your lawyer must be able to trust and respect you.

It took me years to figure out that every lawyer is not like me. My clients bake me cookies and bring me pictures of their grandkids. I, in turn, lose sleep over the best way to resolve my clients' problems. I even tell my clients, when they sign up, "If someone is going to lose sleep over this, let it be me. That's my job, and that's why you are hiring me. So you can sleep." When I get a new client who will never walk again, or never see again, or whose kid was killed by a drunk driver, I never see dollar signs. In the scheme of things, I will have handled thousands of cases before my legal career is over. One case will never "make" me, just as no one case will "break" me, as a lawyer. When I get a big, important case, I see tragedy. Other lawyers say, "Really? You got THAT case? Wow! You are so lucky." But I don't feel lucky. I feel sad for the tragedy and in awe of the responsibility I have to do right by my client. Even on the small cases I am acutely aware of my client's dependence on me to do the right things. I learned a long time ago that no matter how many clients I have, to each client her matter is the most important one.

That is one of the two most important principles that must be understood between your lawyer and you. *Whether your lawyer has a caseload of two or two hundred, your case is the only one that matters to you.* If your lawyer doesn't understand that, he is not the right lawyer for you. A woman hired me recently because I didn't brag to her about how many other big important cases I was handling, like another lawyer had. She told me, "I don't care what you do for anyone else, I just want to know you will do the best possible job for me." That is a good rule to use in hiring a lawyer. Find one you will trust to do the best possible job for you and whose abilities you respect. You can tell a lot about a lawyer in one meeting. Is the lawyer ready for you when you arrive, or does she keep you waiting? Does she have her calls held for the duration of your meeting, and does she give you her undivided attention? Does she come across as professional? If she comes across as slovenly or poorly spoken in her meeting with you, how will she come across in court, or in negotiations, or whatever the appropriate forum is? Does she rush you? If she doesn't have time to answer your questions, maybe she is too busy to handle your matter. This applies to the closing of a "simple" residential home sale as well as to "complex" multi-million-dollar commercial litigation. If your lawyer causes the sale of your home to be delayed, how will you close on the purchase of the "dream house" you are already contracted to purchase?

Each case is unique. In some cases, my very representation of an individual is so important it will make the difference between a fed and sheltered family and a hungry and homeless one. I take that responsibility very seriously, and also personally. I understand that other lawyers think it's queer that my clients love me and I love them. I guess I could sleep better if I didn't care so much. If only I saw them as cases and not as people. But they appreciate the care I give them and I appreciate being appreciated. Every time I think I don't want to practice law anymore, maybe get into a less tragedy-filled profession, a client from ten years ago sends me her daughter or granddaughter with an instruction that "Margaret will take good care of you." How can I say no? Is your lawyer someone you would trust to take care of the people most important in your life? Well, you're about as important as people come, in the scheme of things, and you deserve to have the best possible lawyer.

At one time, I had six lawyers representing me on six different matters. None of my lawyers cared about me as much as I care about my clients. I always felt that mine was just another case to the lawyer, although each was VERY important to me. Maybe it's because they are older and more cynical. Maybe it is because they are men. I can't generalize. I suppose it is hard to represent a fellow-lawyer, though I try not to second-guess my lawyers. What do I have a lawyer for, after all? Some lawyers would prefer you believe otherwise, but in *every* case *your lawyer works for you*, and not the other way around. YOU make all the decisions.

Lawyers are sometimes referred to as Counselors at Law. This is for a very good reason. Lawyers provide counsel. We advise people and then we act on the decisions of our clients.

As an attorney, I may be jumping up and down, excited at what I believe to be a generous offer from an insurance company to settle a case, but if the client says the deal is a "no go," then it doesn't happen. End of story.

Now you know the most important thing about working with a lawyer. You are the boss. If a lawyer does not understand the nature of the relationship, then she is not the right lawyer for you. It doesn't matter how many cases like yours the lawyer has handled or where the lawyer went to school or if the lawyer plays golf with the judge. (OK, the last one might be a little important.) The lawyer works for the client. No other arrangement is EVER acceptable.

I met with a lawyer once whom I considered hiring to represent me in a litigation matter. He had been recommended to me by another lawyer as having handled other cases like mine. In the first meeting he actually said to me, "I know you are a lawyer, but if you hire me then I am the lawyer and you are *just the client*, and

I make all the decisions." Now, think about that. Who is paying whom?

Because the client pays the lawyer, the lawyer is employed by the client. That makes the client boss. As in any employee/employer relationship, the boss can reasonably expect certain things from the employee. The client/employer/boss (you) decides the nature of a relationship, just as an employer in the business world defines the job responsibilities. Any lawyer worth her salt understands the nature of the relationship and her status as employee. Each client is different and so makes the rules which make her comfortable. Dealing with the legal system can be frustrating and even overwhelming when you don't understand it. It can be frustrating even when you do understand it. So, *the first rule of hiring a lawyer is to make sure the lawyer understands that she works for you.*

Make sure your lawyer understands what is expected of her. Some clients want to be apprised of the status of their matter twice a week. They want to see every piece of correspondence that comes into and every letter that goes out from the lawyer's office. They want to attend every status hearing and they want regular phone calls. They like their hands held, and this is their right. The number one reason clients fire lawyers is that their lawyers don't return their phone calls. Every phone call from you to your lawyer should be returned promptly. (You must cut your lawyer some slack in this department, though. If your lawyer is usually good about getting back to you but is on trial, then getting back to you the day after your call or even after a few days must still be considered prompt. You want your lawyer concentrating on the matter she is currently focused on, just as you would expect her to focus primarily on YOUR matter when it comes up for trial, arbitration, negotiation, etc.)

Some clients don't want to be bothered with the details. "Let me know if you need something from me, and let me know when it's over." When I am the client, I am this kind of client. In my practice I assume my clients do not want to be bothered with the day-to-day details of their cases unless they tell me otherwise. My clients know I care about them and they trust me to do my best on their cases, and I do. The client needs to be clear about her expectations of the lawyer, and make sure the lawyer understands what the client's needs are. Frustrations creep up on both the client and the lawyer when the client doesn't get what he needs from the lawyer. Lawyers want happy clients. Just like employees want happy bosses. If you want to see copies of letters and orders, tell your lawyer. Otherwise, your lawyer may feel, as I usually do, that you, the client, don't want to bothered with the minutiae. When I have a lawyer representing me, it irritates me when my lawyer sends me copies of letters from his opposing counsel telling me what a lousy person I am and how weak my case is. That is why I have a lawyer. A lawyer is more than an advocate. A lawyer is a buffer. I don't mind my lawyer calling me and telling me, "Those dopes think you're a lousy person and you have a weak case," because I know my lawyer thinks they are dopes and my lawyer is on my side. I believe the number one reason people hire lawyers is so they don't have to deal with the dopes. Nobody wants to listen to an insurance adjuster say, "Oh, you've been off work for a week already. Everyone else with your injury is back to work by now, so you must be a malingerer." We would rather have the adjuster deal with our lawyer, who will tell the adjuster where to put it (nicely, of course).

So, you can see why it is important to choose wisely if you decide you need a lawyer. Your lawyer is your personal warrior. She looks out for you, and you, in turn, are at your lawyer's mercy to do the best possible job for you. As often as I have heard a lawyer joke (yes, as a matter of fact, I do think I know them all!), I have heard grown men whipping out their lawyers' business cards and exclaiming, "My lawyer is better than your lawyer." We hate lawyers, in general, but we love our own. Kind of like, "Kill all the lawyers . . . except mine!"

When to Hire a Lawyer

If you think you need a lawyer, you probably do. If you are feeling underinformed or overwhelmed, you probably are. That may sound too simple, but it is true. I am a lawyer and I can hold my own in almost any situation. I am a pit bull for my clients, but sometimes, when my personal affairs are at issue, my emotions come into play. In those cases, I hire a lawyer, for the same reason my clients hire me. As I explained in the chapter on negotiations, it is always easier to negotiate for someone else than for yourself. And it is easier to sleep when someone else is handling it. So, if you are losing sleep over some matter of concern to you . . . whether it is a dispute with a neighbor or the negotiation of a contract, or what will happen to Aunt Edna's china when you die, then hire a lawyer. If you felt good about handling it, you'd be sleeping well and you would not need a lawyer. I hope that makes sense because I believe every word of it, and that is why I have had as many as six lawyers representing me.

It is said that "A lawyer who represents herself has a fool for a client." That is not always the case, but in general it is true. I can do my own will. As we saw in the last chapter, you can do your own will, too. If you are comfortable doing your own will, go for it. If you're not, GO SEE A LAWYER. That's it. If you think you need a lawyer, then get one!

So, while I am perfectly happy that I did my own will, I had a lawyer each time I bought a home. I am not a real estate lawyer, and every closing I have ever attended had more documents than the one before. I feel more comfortable having a lawyer sit at my elbow and explain each document to me before I affix my John Hancock. If I want to sue someone who owes me money, I do it myself, because suing is what I do best. If someone sued me, I would probably hire a lawyer, because otherwise, I would want to go break the neck of the person who sued me. It is safer for me to have a lawyer, in that case.

It is probably safe for you to represent yourself in traffic court if you have a ticket for speeding or disobeying a stop sign. If, on the other hand, you were arrested for Driving Under the Influence or striking a pedestrian, you need a lawyer. Speeding and stop sign violations have fines as possible penalties. DUI could mean jail time. Similarly, you might be able to go to court by yourself to enforce a child support award, if your ex-husband misses a payment. But do NOT do your own child custody matter. If you lost your life would be altered forever, so of course you would want to have a lawyer who was familiar with child custody and would do the best possible job for you.

If you're losing sleep, feeling pressured or overwhelmed, or if you are facing some great possible consequence from a negative outcome, then GET A LAWYER.

How to Hire a Lawyer

Yellow pages are not the best way to find a lawyer. I hope this comes as a surprise to no one. People who would NEVER think to find a doctor in the yellow pages hire lawyers from there. I, in fact, get most of my business from the yellow pages. (Must be my picture!) In the old days it used to shock me that people would choose me to represent them on an important matter based on an ad I paid money to have printed in the phone book. It doesn't shock me anymore, but I am telling you now, don't do it. Anyone can advertise anything in the yellow pages. The same is true of any advertising—T.V., radio, direct mail.

The law does not recognize specialties, as a rule. Unlike physicians, who get board certified in obstetrics, pediatrics, etc., we lawyers don't have boards. We can advertise that we practice in any legal area. There are no competency tests to pass. So, I could decide tomorrow that I don't want to try cases anymore, and I could put an ad in the yellow pages (or the newspaper, or on T.V. or the radio), and I could say, "Real Estate Closings" or "Trusts." It does not mean I have ever done one before. I might even put in my ad, "Fifteen years experience." It still does not mean I have ever done a single real estate closing or trust. Some lawyers list seventeen areas of the law that they concentrate in. Trust me on this . . . NO ONE can effectively practice in seventeen different areas of the law.

Do not hire a lawyer you have not met. The only exception is when it is absolutely necessary, because you need a lawyer in another part of the country, and you just can't get there to meet one. In that case, do your best to check out the lawyer and ALWAYS interview the lawyer on the phone. If you can, interview more than one lawyer on the phone before choosing, because you can learn a lot about a lawyer by how she addresses your concerns.

A resource called "Martindale-Hubbell" is a good way to check out the background of a lawyer you are considering. Every community library in the country has one. It is a multi-volume directory of lawyers. It is also on the Internet at www.lawyers.com. It tells little things like when a lawyer was born, and when she was licensed to practice law, and where she went to law school and what her area of practice is. Sometimes it will give additional information like representative clients, and associations to which the lawyer belongs. For example, many personal injury lawyers are active in the Association of Trial Lawyers of America. There are other associations for divorce lawyers, estate planning lawyers, and so forth. Group participation is not a guarantee of competence, but belonging helps lawyers stay abreast of current legal issues.

The best way to find a lawyer, of course, is by personal referral. The best people to refer you are other professionals. If you had a lawyer prepare a will for you, and you now need a lawyer to represent you on an employment matter, call your lawyer!! Lawyers know lawyers, both by reputation and personally. A lawyer can refer you to the person she would call if she had your same problem. If you don't know a lawyer, ask another professional. Your accountant would be a good person to ask. Finally, ask your friends and neighbors. Ask your coworkers. If someone you know was in a car accident and filed suit, ask if he was happy with the lawyer he used and the outcome of his case. Ask if he would recommend his lawyer. Get more than one name if you can, and then consider your candidates.

Make an appointment to see one or more than one. Some lawyers will want to talk to you on the phone first, just to make sure your problem is something she handles. This is a good thing, because it saves both of you time. If you want to bring an age discrimination case against your employer, you want someone who does age discrimination cases and not just sex discrimination cases, for example. In most cases, a lawyer who is unable or unwilling to take on your case can refer you to another lawyer who can help you.

What should you expect from the first meeting? First of all, do NOT pay for an initial consultation. Make sure to ask when you make the appointment whether the lawyer charges for an initial consultation. Almost all lawyers give short free consultations. This is because you cannot be expected to hire a lawyer before you have met him. So, you meet. Check each other out. You set forth your expectations of the lawyer, and the lawyer tells you what he can do for you. Have all your questions prepared for the first meeting. Has the lawyer handled cases like your before? What kind of outcome does he think you can expect in your case? If you are the kind of client who likes regular status reports, will this lawyer oblige you? How much will he charge you? Is it to be an hourly rate, or a flat fee, or a contingent fee? Contingent fees are most common in personal injury cases, and most often the lawyer gets one-third of the client's ultimate recovery, by settlement or at trial. Do not sign anything at the initial consultation with the lawyer. Have the lawyer send you a fee agreement (or give you one to take home). Read it and discuss it with the people with whom you discuss your other important decisions. If you have questions, call the lawyer and ask. For example, if the contract says that the client is responsible for expenses, like copying and postage, ask the lawyer how much he expects the expenses to be. Then, if you like the lawyer, and if you trust that he will do the best possible job for you and you feel that he respects you, hire him. Make sure you understand what to expect of your lawyer and what he expects of you. If you have any reservations, or if you will lose sleep about your decision to hire this lawyer, don't do it. There are about a gazillion lawyers in the United States. Find the one who is best for you.

I want to tell you a secret that most lawyers do not want you to know. Bar association referral services are about the worst places to find lawyers. They are worse than yellow pages. Each bar association has a revolving card file of lawyers in each practice area. Take bankruptcy as an example. For a hundred dollars, or fifty or a thousand, depending on the association, I can list myself with a bar association as a bankruptcy lawyer. I can also list myself as a real estate lawyer, workers' compensation lawyer, copyright lawyer, and on and on. As many lists as I am willing to pay to be on, they will put me on, without regard to whether I know a darn thing about that area of law. They use the money the lawyers pay to advertise the referral service, and then when a prospective client calls, she is given the next name in the revolving card file and then the succeeding name moves to the top of the card file. This is how the referral services are SUPPOSED to work, at any rate. Sometimes unscrupulous lawyers manipulate the system. We had a scandal here in my practice area in which the president of the local bar association kicked money back to the administrator of the referral service to send him the best cases. In another case, four or six local lawyers started up their own "bar association" so they could advertise "referral services" and keep all the business for themselves. Smart idea for them. Bad idea for their clients. So, unless you absolutely cannot find a lawyer any other way (for example, if your case is in a very uncommon practice area), do not call your local bar association.

When Should You Fire Your Lawyer?

The answer to the question, "When should you fire your lawyer" is "almost never." I'm sorry if that sounds self-serving, but it is my experience that it is almost never in the client's best interest to change lawyers mid-stream. Your lawyer knows your case better than anyone else. Even if you come to regret your choice of lawyers, unless your lawyer is truly incompetent or uncaring, the lawyer you have is better, at least for the case at hand, than a fresh one. If you want to change lawyers, do it for the next case. There are several reasons for this. First, changing lawyers is expensive. If you are paying by the hour and your lawyer spends twenty hours investigating and learning a case for you, you do not want to pay another lawyer to spend twenty hours acquainting herself with the same case. Secondly, let's say your lawyer is representing you in an adversarial situation, like a divorce. If your spouse's lawyer has been on the case from the beginning (and sat through the depositions and hearings), then his lawyer will have an advantage over your newly hired lawyer. Finally, when you change lawyers you lose continuity and sometimes credibility. So if you are negotiating the purchase of a business and your lawyer makes certain gains and certain concessions, and then you hire a new lawyer who doesn't know the history of the negotiations, the deal might get bogged down or even killed.

Almost never is not the same as never. Notice I did not say never fire a lawyer. Just like employers would like to never fire an employee (for a lot of reasons), lucky clients never have to fire their lawyers. But sadly, employers do sometimes have to fire employees (for lots of reasons) and sometimes clients must fire lawyers. When there is no trust or respect between the client and lawyer, there is no workable relationship. In that case you are better with no lawyer than with one in whom you have lost faith. If your lawyer lies to you, you should fire him. Similarly, though, if you lie to your lawyer, your lawyer should fire you as a client.

If, after seeing your lawyer in action, *you are sure* your lawyer is not competent to handle the matter you have entrusted to her, fire her. No point going down with a sinking ship. In the case that you have lost confidence in your lawyer's abilities to represent you, you must fire your lawyer. It's the old lost sleep notion. I know what it is to lose sleep worrying whether your lawyer will handle your case in a competent manner. But the point of having a lawyer was to allow you to sleep. Keeping a lawyer who is incompetent (to your way of thinking—this does not mean the lawyer is incompetent, but only that you don't feel confidence in her) is a losing proposition. And from experience I can tell you, your instinct on this is usually right. If you think your lawyer is going to lose your case, she probably will. Better to write off the fees you paid her and hire someone else.

It may also be necessary to fire a lawyer who neglects you. In this instance it may even be possible to get your fees back. If you have repeatedly left unanswered messages with your lawyer; if he never calls and never responds to your requests for information, then you must fire him. An unresponsive lawyer is as useful as no lawyer at all. Understand that lawyers are people, too. We get busy. The fact of the matter is, though your case is most important of all, we have other clients and other cases. I have had clients call me at 7 A.M. on a Sunday with a routine question (as opposed to an emergency), and then get mad that I didn't call back till Monday morning. I have a life. If those clients fire me, it's fine with me. (They usually don't though. They're not that sensitive.) A lawyer knows when her relationship with her client is strained, and usually when a lawyer gets fired she is not surprised.

The final reason to fire a lawyer is the one ABSOLUTELY, POSITIVELY MUST FIRE situation. And that is when the lawyer drops the ball. If your lawyer does not show up for court hearings, depositions, negotiating sessions, or other events important to your matter, or if he fails to file important documents in court, then you must fire him. Continuing on with a lawyer who is obviously not representing your interests is like pointing an unloaded gun at a burglar. If the burglar has a loaded gun, you're a dead woman. If your lawyer is unprepared, unresponsive, or incompetent, and your matter is an important one, your case is lost. You're a dead woman.

How does one accomplish the firing? A letter works best. All you need say is "I've decided to seek representation elsewhere. Please forward my file." Even easier is having the new lawyer write the letter requesting the file from the fired one.

When to Do It Yourself (And How To)

There is a term for people who represent themselves in legal matters. *Pro se* simply means "for yourself." So, when you file a lawsuit or defend one, *pro se*, it means you are doing it yourself, without a lawyer. Even a lawyer who represents herself in court is considered *pro se*. Most jurisdictions have *pro se* courts. They are courts of small claims in which no one has a lawyer. Usually cases under five hundred or a thousand dollars are directed to *pro se* court. The theory behind *pro se* court is that the amount in controversy is so small that hiring a lawyer would defeat the purpose of pursuing the claim at all. In the United States, each party pays his own attorney's fees. This is different from the British system, in which the losing party pays his own lawyer and the lawyer of the winner. So, in our system, it is possible to win your case and still "lose" if the attorney's fees exceed the award.

There are two reasons to act as your own attorney—choice and necessity. If you feel confident you can handle the matter at hand without a lawyer, then you can. You might feel confident to negotiate a second lease after having had a lawyer do the first one. The same principles apply to other contracts. If you have a lawyer review the contracts in the first place, you will know what to look for in future contracts.

After reading this book you will know how to find appropriate forms to do wills, leases, and other legal documents. Those forms exist specifically to help you do it yourself. Feel free to. This is an example of acting *pro se* by choice. Many people prefer to do it themselves and spend the saved attorney's fees on a vacation. Other people are not comfortable acting without a lawyer, and by all means, there are plenty of lawyers ready and willing to take their money.

Keep in mind that very rarely should you feel you MUST represent yourself. In criminal matters, a lawyer will be appointed for you in the event you cannot afford one. This applies only in cases in which your life or liberty are at stake . . . if you can go to jail if your are convicted, you are entitled to a public defender if you cannot otherwise afford an attorney. If only money is at stake—a fine, no matter how substantial—the court will NOT appoint you an attorney. A criminal record is something that will stick with you, so get an attorney for all but the most innocuous criminal matters. Do your own jaywalking or littering case. Do not do your own embezzlement, shoplifting, or other criminal cases that might result in jail time. If you don't have a job you will probably qualify for a public defender. If you do have a job, beg or borrow if you have to, and get a lawyer.

See Chapter Ten for resources for people who need a lawyer in a civil matter but can't afford one.

If you do decide to represent yourself, especially in court, here are some important tips. Treat everyone with respect. Treat the clerks with respect and treat your opposing party or his attorney with respect. You will go much farther if you are civil with people in life and in the legal system. Every successful lawyer treats her opposing counsel, and every party in the case, with respect. We might even beat the rhetorical daylights out of each other in court, but then we might go have a cup of coffee. Clients are always amazed to find out my opposing counsel and I actually like each other, despite our differences. Win or lose, we respect each other. We all work hard to be good lawyers and we respect the hard work of our adversaries. Over the years I have had many new clients referred to me by lawyers who opposed me on a previous case. I have also had clients referred to me by doctors whose depositions I have taken, and even by defendants who were sued by me. Universally they say, "I was really impressed by the way you handled yourself." It really is nothing more than treating them demandingly but with RESPECT. We can scream at each other on the phone sometimes but then we always say, "Have a good weekend," or, "I am glad you are feeling better. I know you were sick last time I talked to you."

There is another reason to treat your adversary with respect. He will like it. Why is that important? If you are negotiating a settlement, and you just need that extra thousand dollars to close the deal, he will be far more likely to try to get if for you if you have treated him with respect and not like trash.

Why is it important to treat every clerk at the courthouse with respect? Think about it. You get nothing done at the courthouse without the help of a clerk. They can pull your file now, or they call pull your file when they get done helping everyone else in line. They can call your case first, or they can call it after that big-ugly-hairy used car deal case they know will take all morning.

You already know why you should treat the judge with respect. "Your Honor" is the appropriate name to call a judge in court. Not "Hey," or "Yeah," or even "Judge." They get to wear the robes. You get to call them "Your Honor." Yes, they really do care. You would, too. If you are in *pro se* court, the proceedings will seem to be directly out of the "People's Court." The judge will listen to each side in turn and rule. No special treatment for anyone. If you are in another court and you do not have a lawyer, the court will bend over backward to accommodate you. Judges know it is hard even for lawyers to maneuver though cases, and so they will help you. The one thing no one but a lawyer can do for you is give you legal advice. The judge will not advise you how to handle your case. The clerks cannot advise you either. They can only tell you what papers you need to file, and when the case will be heard—logistical things. If you decide to do a case without a lawyer, make sure you do your research! Then, go get 'em. Don't let anyone intimidate you, and don't back down. After all, you know you're right. Right?

Pro Se Help

When you are handling a legal matter by yourself, do not forget all the resources that are available to you.

Ask questions of the court clerks, if you are doing a court case by yourself, either as Plaintiff or Defendant. Find out if the cases usually go to trial on the first date or if they are usually continued. Find out if you can present evidence by affidavit or if you need to bring witnesses. If you are doing your own case in court, ask the clerk what forms and resources are available directly from the court. Do not worry that you will sound dumb. Act as dumb as possible. They will feel sorry for you and help you more. Even I do that. I call the clerk of the court and I say, in my most helpless voice, "Hi, can you HELP me? I've never done this before. I don't know where to start." I don't even care if they think I'm dumb. I just want to get the job done. So should you. Ask for help. Don't demand it. Be polite and be APPRECIATIVE.

Here in Cook County we have a booklet that is put out by the court system that explains how *pro se* court works. The booklet is free for the asking. We also have a bar association attorney available to answer questions at the courthouse one afternoon a week for *pro se* litigants. The forms for complaint and summons are available from the clerk of court, but because the clerk cannot provide legal advice, the clerk cannot always answer all your questions about how to fill out the forms. Find out if *pro se* help is available.

8

What Men Have Always Known and Women Are Just Learning

(NETWORKING 101)

My dictionary is so old, it gives four definitions of "network," and they're all nouns. Network has definitely become a verb. Just like woodworkers make things out of wood and lace makers make lace, networkers make *nets*. And what is a net good for? Just ask a Flying Wallenda! We all need a net as we maneuver the high wire of life. We need one so that if we fall we will not hit pavement. We need them to support us in tough times.

Keep in mind that you acquire the networks of everyone in your network. You don't need to know everyone in town, you just need to know somebody who knows somebody who can help you when you need help.

You don't need to know Michael Jordan to get his autograph on a ball for your charity's bazaar, you just need to know his wife's golf teacher, or kids' soccer coach, or mom's neighbor. (OK. Nobody really knows anybody who really knows Michael Jordan, but you get my drift.) So how do you get to know people who can help you when you need help? And how do you know who these people are? Well, you want people in your network who have big and helpful networks of their own.

"Important" in this sense doesn't mean that they ARE Michael Jordan or that they are CEO of a multinational corporation, or even president of the local bank. "Important" in networking means people who are *willing as well as able* to help you. Some people don't help anybody. They look out for number one and not numbers two through two thousand (*you*). You don't need these people in your network, even if they own the *Fortune* 500. You need people you can call and say, "Hi, it's Kate. Help!" and they won't laugh, or hang up, or say "Gotta go. Chat later." There are friends, and then there are friends, as every woman knows. The people in your network need not be your best friends. It's not necessary that they come to your kids' recitals or that they invite you over for Sunday brunch. It's enough that they know you and that you know you can count on them.

So who are these people and how do you find them? Read on.

Networking Clubs Do Not Work

Networking as a catch phrase has only been hot for about fifteen years. So, for about fifteen years, something called Networking Groups have been multiplying like rabbits. They have names like

LEADS Club, and Breakfast to Network; some are part of national organizations and some are local. Many are women-only and some are coed. I've never heard of a men-only networking group. This could be because the Supreme Court would laugh, or because men know that networking for the sake of networking is generally a waste of time.

If you've ever been to a networking club, you'll understand my reference instantly. I've sampled a few of these groups' meetings, but never more than once, and they inevitably work like this: The group (usually between a dozen and twenty people) sit on the outsides of a group of tables arranged in a circle. They share a meal, usually breakfast or lunch. While the meal is being served, the president or leader asks each member and guest to introduce herself and tell what kinds of leads (or referrals) she's seeking. They pass their business cards around the table, each person taking one or two of each.

They finish eating and then they go around and introduce themselves *again*. I've never understood this because my memory stretches way past the half hour it takes to eat a plate of eggs, but they do it. Does it work? Well, it works for me in that I've met a dozen or twenty people when it's over. But, inevitably, in each of these groups you will find one Mary Kay Cosmetics representative, one insurance saleswoman, one realtor, one printer, one interior decorator, one mortgage broker, and maybe even one lawyer. Do I want to eat with them again next week? Not on your life. Am I a snob? Hah! I'm busy. I'm thriving. I don't have time for that networking stuff.

Networking groups don't work because successful people don't need to network with people who are looking to network. And, they don't have time to. But the people who are already successful and thriving are the ones you want in your network. Bank presidents are too busy to belong to networking groups. They send loan officers and trust administrators to the networking clubs. The president does her networking in more meaningful ways.

Networking clubs are ineffective because they're limited. Think about it. The same group meets every week. Not only do I not need to be introduced to Mary Mortgage twice in one morning, I don't need to be introduced to her again every week. I certainly don't need to collect two of her cards every week. And I don't need to give her two of mine.

Networking clubs inevitably have memberships. You're expected to join, which costs money, and you are expected to come to lunch every week. Now, why would I want to pay money to belong to an organization that takes my time and makes me meet the same twenty people over and over and over again? This, to me, is not networking. Men just wouldn't waste the time. Women don't seem to have a problem with it because their moms did it. They didn't call it networking, though. They called it a coffee klatch. Don't confuse the two. If you want to get together with a group of women over finger sandwiches and small talk, feel free. Don't invite me; I'm busy networking the old-fashioned way . . . the way men have always done it and women are just learning to do.

Service Organizations

I used to be one of those women who said, "If men want to have men's clubs, let them. Women, after all, have women's clubs." Excuse me while I slap myself upside the head.

Great networking takes place at what used to be exclusively male organizations. Before women were allowed to join, all the good networking took place "just between the boys." Rotary clubs are a good example. Starting in 1905, for eighty years, women were excluded from Rotary. We'd probably still be excluded if the

U.S. Supreme Court hadn't ordered Rotary to let us in. Why is this important?

Rotary, Jaycees, Kiwanis, and Lions are the best service *and* networking opportunities around. Their members work together to make their town, country, and world better. They throw fundraisers, which require meeting and planning and laughing and arguing together. They work together toward common goals. They clean up roadsides and paint senior citizens' houses. They hold blood drives and holiday parties and auctions and picnics and outings for the members. They know each others' spouses and they announce weddings and births at their meetings. If one of them dies, the whole club shows up at the funeral. Why? Because members of these groups are profoundly connected to each other. And that is what networking is all about.

Members of service organizations become friends. So, if a member of Lions knows someone who needs a mortgage she can recommend someone in her Lions club. Why is this different from recommending someone in a networking club? Because two Lions have worked side by side over weeks and years to accomplish mutual goals in service. Two networkers only ate eggs together. A service club member may not have done BUSINESS with another member of the club, but she can vouch for the member nonetheless. Why? She'll know that the member returns her phone calls. She'll know that when she undertakes a project she follows through. She'll know a little something about her family and where she lives and whether she works full-time as a mortgage broker, or if she's really a house painter who sells mortgages now and then.

Another benefit of service organizations is that they are very often international. Lions, Rotary, Kiwanis, and Jaycees all are. Lions clubs have a program for collecting and distributing eyeglasses all over the world. Kiwanis clubs are combating iodine deficiency, the world over. Rotarians have given millions of dollars and thousands of volunteer hours to immunize every child in the world against polio, so that polio will be *eradicated*, not just in our lifetimes, but within the next few years. Being part of a global service group makes you part of something very important, and gives you friends in every conceivable faraway place.

I have attended Rotary club meetings in a dozen U.S. states and a dozen foreign countries. By doing so I have increased my network tremendously. I will never be a stranger in a strange place because I have Rotary friends on every continent, with whom I can share a meal as well as fellowship and knowledge. This is a wonderful new opportunity for women, and women should take advantage.

So how do you decide which club to join, expand, or start? Well, what kind of service are you interested in? Who do you want to meet while you're doing it? How much time do you have to devote to it? Find out what the time commitments are for each organization and find out who in town belongs. Find out how much it costs (all clubs have some sort of dues). Don't forget that you will be expected to contribute to fund-raisers, as well.

Many local newspapers list various clubs' meetings on a weekly or daily basis. Usually the name and number of a person to contact is included in the listing. The Internet is also a good source of information about any national or international group. All service organizations have web sites. Just remember that charitable groups' web sites are usually located at dot "org" and not dot "com" or dot "net."

Most service organizations and clubs require sponsorship by a member. I became the first woman in my local Rotary Club through a client. He had met his previous lawyer in Rotary, he told me. So I asked what Rotary was all about. I was interested, and my client offered to take me to a meeting and sponsor me if I wanted to join. The sponsorship requirement is good for your network. It results in a high-quality membership. Your fellow Rotarian is likely to be a decision-maker in her business—the president of the bank and not a teller—because membership is something of an honor.

There are ways to find sponsors. Call the organization and ask if they have open houses or membership drives or other means of meeting members for sponsorship. Your friends and colleagues may have information about clubs as well.

Attend a few meetings of a club you might want to join and see if you fit in. You might decide not to join, but you'll have met some nice people.

When I had been in Rotary for a year, someone asked me if I got business from being in Rotary. I had to think about it. I got so wrapped up in doing service (it is an addictive good feeling to do good work) that I'd forgotten that I joined to get business. I got a great network of great people who care about people. In Rotary we are forbidden to discuss our personal businesses at club meetings. Lions and Kiwanians have similar rules. A tenet of Lions is that "no club shall hold out the financial betterment of its members as its object." The financial betterment of its members is a bonus, though, as any Lion will tell you.

Do you see now what you get in a service organization that you don't get in a networking club? You get a real, honest to goodness *network*. Sure, you don't talk shop at the meetings. You get to know each other—which is better.

The point is that networking for networking's sake does not work. The point is that you should get involved in doing something important—important to you, but also important in your community or in the scheme of things. Take up a cause. If you feel strongly about guns, join your local NRA. If you are a dog lover, get on the board of your local pet shelter. You will meet like-minded people who will be impressed with your energy and enthusiasm. Which brings me to another point about networking. There is no point in just belonging. Just belonging to a group will get you on a mailing list, which is, of course, not networking.

If you decide a ski club is going to be a good networking place for you, then go to the meetings. Take one of the trips or at least get on a committee. Go to the holiday party, but better yet, get on the holiday party planning committee. You don't need to be passing out your cards. Trust me on this. If you are an active and effective member of a group, the other members will know who you are. Even without a card your fellow members will know to call you for their next mortgage or printing job or Mary Kay consultation, whichever the case may be.

Special Interest Clubs

Where are the people *you* want to meet? Maybe you have a hobby or pastime you really enjoy. There's probably a club for it that you can join. You may find it easier to get your networking feet wet by joining a club for an activity that interests you.

My local paper lists available options. I was astounded at the choices. There are clubs for enthusiasts of all kinds: photographers, colored pencil artists, decorative painters, square dancers, country and western dancers, Tai Chi practitioners, Daughters of the American Revolution, amateur radio operators, Civil War re-enactors, sewers, chess players, runners, home-brewers, GI Joe collectors, writers, scuba divers, Toastmasters, and hundreds more.

Try going where your interests lie, but consider whether the group is one that you would choose to include in your network because everyone you meet is a potential cog in your wheel and you are a potential cog in theirs.

Some special interest groups will be better for networking than others. If you are looking for people with money to network with, you might want to consider an opera guild or a polo club. On the other hand, if opera makes you doze, don't waste your time. You won't have anything to talk about once you get there and no one will care to network with you.

Let's say you are a high-priced couturier who likes long bike rides. You might want to join a biking group, of course. But if you live on the poor side of town you might want to join the group across town. Hmm. This sounds snobby even to me, but when you reach the resting point on a long ride and you want to talk about what you do, you'll be sorry you didn't choose a group that can relate to what you want to talk about. If you're not going to chat, you might as well ride alone!

Professional Organizations

If your goal is to network with people in your field, then a professional organization is for you. Lawyers have bar associations. Nurses, paralegals, dental hygenists, and mortgage bankers also have groups. But before you decide to spend all your available networking time with people who do exactly what you do, ask yourself what you expect to get out of belonging to such an organization. If you want support—someone who will listen and commiserate when you talk about your profession—then great. For example, I started a group of literary agents in Chicago, called CLAS—Chicago Literary Agents Society. I felt that we were somewhat isolated from the big publishing activity going on in New York, and that if we didn't hang together, we would hang separately. We network really well, and we are supportive of each other. If another Chicago agent calls me and says, "I have this book but I don't know where to send it," I'll offer suggestions. The literary agents in my group refer each other manuscripts that we aren't able to or interested to represent.

Friends of mine who are employed by big corporations belong

to professional organizations like "Women in Transportation" and "The Association of Purchasing Professionals." Groups like that network by keeping each other abreast of changes within their industries. If a new packaging material comes on the market, a purchasing manager might first learn of it through one of these organizations. Friendships are also created in these groups, and if, for example, a member loses her job, she might be able to find another job through the network she created in a professional association.

If, on the other hand, you own your own business and your goal is to build your clientele, this might not be the way to go. For example, I first joined the local bar association thinking I would get referrals from other lawyers in my community who don't do what I do. The joke was on me, I guess, because the lawyers in my local bar association coveted what business I had and weren't about to share any of theirs with me.

Every group and profession differs. Go to a few meetings of any group you are thinking about joining before you ante up. Most groups will let you visit a few times before you decide to join. Meet the people. Get a feeling for the group and the benefits and commitments involved. Then decide. If you don't join, you won't have wasted your time. You'll have met some people who might become part of your network.

Support and Health-Oriented Groups

I'm not going to spend a lot of time talking about these groups. They exist for people who need them. Alcoholics Anonymous, La Leche, Overeaters Anonymous, Y-Me for Breast Cancer support—the list here is long. Join one of these groups for what the group can do for you. If you need support or information, go get it, by all means. This is not a networking group per se, but support and information are a benefit of networking. Finding a person who has been where you are can be tremendously comforting and beneficial. Women in these groups sometimes form lifelong friendships, which is good any way you look at it.

This is one networking variety women do better than men. Far more women participate in breast cancer support than men do prostate cancer support, for example. Maybe men think seeking support is a sign of weakness. Thank goodness women don't have that problem.

Faith Networking

It didn't occur to me to include this category until I talked to a pastor friend, but some of you are apparently doing your business networking at church. Hmm. I don't really have a problem with this—much. According to my friend, some people join a church, get the church directory, and then use it as a direct marketing campaign tool for their insurance business, real estate business, dental practice, and the like. You can decide for yourself whether this is a good idea. My preference would be that if you are going to network at church, you get involved in the church—do some teaching, serve on a committee, join a sisterhood.

Do not underestimate the value of faith-based networking. I cannot encourage you to join a church to network—some little, chirpy voice inside my head tells me this is hypocritical. However, I have known local election campaigns that were won because whole churches went out and worked for their fellow parishioner. When the incumbent mayor of a town in my area was defeated by a challenger, the conventional wisdom was that the new mayor's church worked harder then the previous mayor's. I ran for office once against a person of a certain religion, and every church of his faith in town got out the vote for my opponent.

Of course, when I think of church I think of the more traditional networking that goes on there. Churches and synagogues are the best places to form a spiritual network. If a spiritual network is important to you, then join a house of worship that will meet your spiritual needs.

Chambers of Commerce

For business networking, Chambers of Commerce have been a traditional venue. Originally Chambers of Commerce encouraged people and businesses to move to one town as opposed to another. They encouraged people in town to shop locally. They still do these things, but since the 1980s they've devoted more energy to networking among members. Most Chambers of Commerce have monthly Business After Hours, or "Mixers," at which members can congregate and pass out business cards. Chambers of Commerce come in both the local (one town) and regional (e.g., Northwest Suburban) versions. The bigger the region covered by the Chamber, the more members it probably has, and the more people you might be able to meet for your network.

My advice about Chambers of Commerce is to attend a few meetings of several local groups, if there are more than one in your area. Meet the people. Find out what kinds of programs the Chamber offers. If most of their meetings are lunches, and you work retail and cannot get away at lunch, you'll be wasting your money by joining. Also, joining a Chamber of Commerce can be expensive. I tend to rotate my chamber memberships from year to year, because I notice that each Chamber's Business After Hours group attracts the same people month after month. Also, every Chamber allows guests at its events. Sometimes a nonmember will have to pay to attend an event, or pay more than a member would pay, but the difference will still be less than it costs to join.

Private Clubs

Private clubs have always excluded women and minorities. The excluded parties have often started their own clubs because of this. We've all heard stories about prominent members of communities being asked to join clubs and then the club being embarrassed at having to withdraw the invitation to join when it was revealed that the prospective member had a "questionable" parentage . . . part Black or part Jewish or some other inflammatory condition. Whether or not you choose to associate with a club with a history of this is up to you.

What kind of private clubs are there? Generally I mean country clubs. Country clubs abound in the suburbs and in rural areas, although there are some in the big cities of course. There is also another kind of private club. Whereas country clubs emphasize beautifully manicured golf courses and dress codes, in urban areas there are private clubs sans the golf. They have other amenities like exclusive dining rooms, sometimes with spectacular views, and sometimes, health clubs and guest rooms. In Chicago we have the Union League Club and the Metropolitan Club and the Standard Club and many others. Some of these have a cooperative system whereby if you belong to one club you may attend functions at other clubs. Some country clubs have cooperative arrangements too.

How can you tell a private club from a public club? Well, for one thing, membership is by invitation. You must be sponsored by a member and usually some board or committee must vote to approve your membership. More importantly, you must be able to pay the big bucks to buy into the club and then pay the dues, which can also be impressive.

So, why would you want to spend thousands of dollars to belong to a private club (that has only recently started taking women as members even though they didn't really want to)? So you will have access to other people who have so much money they can spend it on a private club so they won't have to associate with the rest of us. Private clubs have private club rosters. They have event nights, and in the case of country clubs, they have golf tournaments. You might join for the amenities. The golf course might be the best in town or it might have more readily accessible tee times. If you are a golfer, use golf as a networking tool. Men have been doing this forever. The rest of your foursome will be impressed if you take them to a hoity-toity country club to golf. If you belong to a private dining club, and you take a prospective business contact to lunch, she will be impressed. I don't need to belong to a private club because all the successful lawyers I know belong to every club in the city. To entice me to send them business, they quite often take me to their private clubs for lunch or dinner. I get all the benefits . . . fancy food, great views, impeccable service . . . and somebody else pays for it. In the old days they acted like I was privileged to be allowed into the place, since women were not included for membership. As long as I get to eat and I don't have to pay, I am happy. However, to many people, you will have arrived on the day that you join a private club. Remember that some of the old coots will resent your being there. Ignore them. I was at a luncheon once at which my seat mates were members of Bob-O-Link Country Club, here in the Chicago area. One old codger was lamenting that if they let women in as members he wouldn't be able to swim in the club's pool naked. Oh, the poor soul.

Make no mistake about it, people in clubs do business together. If you are not wealthy, then joining an expensive private club is not an option. Plus, you have to be sponsored, and that might be a trick in itself if the club is reluctant or refuses to accept women as members. My own United States senator belongs to a local country club that excludes women as members. Nobody seems to care. If you join a club you will have access to other rich people and if rich people figure into your network in a prominent way, then joining a private club might be worth the investment. You should go where you want to be and where the people are with whom you want to network.

Charities

Charity fund-raisers are another way to meet rich people.

Usually the higher the ticket price, the richer the people attending, but not always. You will probably not find poor people at a $200-a-plate event, but you will find all kinds of people at an event for Alzheimer's or cancer because these awful diseases affect so many people that no one can afford to ignore their causes. Even better than attending a fund-raiser for a charity is getting on a charity board. You will meet like-minded, and generally well-thought-of, people in your community. It will not be enough to be on the board, though. You will have to be an active participant if you hope to network effectively on a board. Similarly, you can't just attend a fund-raiser and expect to expand your network . . . you must get out and MINGLE!

New-Fashioned Networking: Inter-networking

Do not discount cyberspace as a place to do effective networking. Nothing beats a face-to-face meeting, complete with a direct gaze and a firm handshake. However, sometimes the people you need to meet are not in your backyard. Or sometimes they *are* in your backyard, but you just don't know it. I first got on-line in 1990. My on-line profile included my name, general location, and profession. A gentleman in my area was writing an article for a trade magazine and wanted to know if he could interview me about how to handle bad home contractors. He had done a member directory search, which I guess he felt was more effective than calling lawyers out of the phone book. I did the interview for him, and we actually stayed in touch for a period of years. He introduced me to chatting on-line, as a matter of fact. He told me about a chat room for writers in which he would spend time.

It strikes me funny now, but this gentleman had to actually call me on the phone and talk me through the process of getting to a chat room. Prior to my contact with this man, I had only used my Internet account to send and receive email. I have to tell you that the first time I visited a chat room, I had no idea what was going on. Little snippets kept scrolling up my screen and I could not figure out who was addressing whom or how anyone kept track. Chatters in the room even gave me cyber-hugs (my name typed within parentheses) and cyber-kisses (my name followed by asterisks). Thank goodness my new friend was on the phone with me (and in the same chat room with me) and he explained all about cyber affection.

I still "hang out" in the writers' chat rooms, and I can tell you that some good networking gets done there. I have taken clients for my literary agency from the pool of writers who spend time in the chats. Regulars in the chats visit each other in real life when they are in each other's towns. There really would be no other way that I know of for all of these people to come together. They exchange writing ideas and publishing contacts and they develop friendships. It's a new but worthwhile development in the networking realm.

Internet bulletin boards are another way to network on-line. You can post a note on any number of message boards located throughout cyberspace. There are thousands of them. You can ask a question or post a comment. You will almost certainly get a response. Millions of users around the world will have access to your post, and someone will have something to say about it. I used to post regularly on the *Chicago Tribune* message boards. As a result I became friends with, among others, Mike Royko. I had posted a message critical of another columnist, and in her defense, Royko posted a message calling me an expletive!

The editor-in-chief of the newspaper emailed me to apologize. I thought it was uproariously funny and I didn't mind being called an expletive by the notoriously cantankerous Royko. I became friends with the editor-in-chief of the paper, and ultimately I became friends with Mike Royko. I sent him a letter and said, "If it's okay with you, I'd like to agree to disagree about that columnist's merits as a columnist; and if it's okay with you, I'd also like to agree to disagree about my status as a (expletive)." Mr. Royko and I chatted on-line almost every day after that. I taught him how to give and receive cyber-hugs. He died owing me lunch. I still miss him.

Something to Think About

If you decide that you want to use a group for networking purposes, consider where you will fit into the organization's power structure. If you are joining a group for fun, then just go and have fun. But if you are joining to meet people who will empower you, then join a group in which you will be neither the most nor least powerful person.

There is an adage in real estate never to buy the most or least valuable home in a neighborhood because it will appreciate less than other homes in the same neighborhood. From my experience, the women with the most and least power in a group stand to gain the least from belonging. This is Margaret's Theory of Networking. If you are the least powerful member of a group, then you have little to offer the other members. If you are a cashier at a small local business and you join a group in which the other members are all presidents of multi-national corporations, then you won't be particularly useful to the other members. I know this sounds cold, but it's true. They're there to network, too. On the other hand, if you are the CEO of a billion-dollar company, and you join a group in which all the other members are entry-level office workers, then most likely they'll want something from you and not have much to give, at least in a traditional business sense. So if you want to network in order to gain resources for acquiring power, join a group of people in which you fit somewhere into the middle of their particular power structure.

Build a House of Cards

Think of business cards as your tickets in the lottery of successful networking. The more tickets you have in the lottery, the greater your chance of hitting it big. So get your cards out there. Your odds of winning in the successful networking lottery are much better than your odds of winning your state's lottery. And she who has the most tickets is most likely to win.

Business cards immediately come to mind when a woman thinks about networking, and no woman should ever be caught without a stack of them. If you are employed, your employer will have provided you with a box or two of cards. Sometimes you'll be issued standard company business cards. Sometimes you'll have some input as to the amount of information on your cards. Trust me, you can't have too much information on your cards. How many different ways can you be reached? Put them all on your cards: phone number, fax number, email address, U.S. mail address. Pager? Telex? Put them on there. Of course, if your employer is generating your business cards, then your employer's logo and information will be on the cards. What if you're generating your own cards? Go crazy!

Get lots and lots of business cards. You can get five hundred black on white cards for between twenty and twenty-five dollars. You can get a second five hundred for ten or twelve dollars more. There is economy of scale anytime you do a printing job. So unless you're planning a move or you expect the phone company to change your area code this year, get tons of cards. They're *cheap*.

What should they look like? If you're printing your own cards, you can put anything you like on them. If you have been networking all along, you will have dozens of sample cards from your contacts already in your collection. Printers also have books of samples. Find a design that's easy to read. Black ink is easy to read, and cheaper. If you feel the need for color, try a colored stock, but you can't go wrong with black ink on white stock.

What information should be on your cards? Well, if you are printing your own cards, you can give yourself any title you like. I think I'd like to have "World's Greatest Lawyer" on my cards. Don't be shy. You think everyone with an important-sounding title is an important person? Well, you're right, so give yourself the most important-sounding title that is appropriate. My sister used to translate brochures for a local anti–drunk driving organization into Spanish. She asked if she could have the title "Director of Hispanic Relations" and, of course, they said yes. So she had that title on her cards, even as a volunteer, and she put it on her resumé, which sounds impressive. What did it cost the charity to give her that title? Nothing. There are some reasonable limitations here, of course. You can't take a title that requires credentials you don't have. "Mary Doe, Brain Surgeon" is out for obvious reasons, unless you have actually buzzed your way into gray matter.

Some women like to make their cards unique by adding their own pictures, or a logo. Either is fine. Pictures make cards more expensive, but they also make them more memorable. Keep in mind, though, that it is generally salespeople who have their pictures on their cards. Realtors do this a lot. Bank presidents never have their pictures on their cards. Some people might think a picture on a card does not present a professional image. Go by the rule of thumb for your profession.

You might also want to put a logo on your cards. Some obvious logos are the scales of justice for a lawyer or a pair of shears for a hair stylist. These can make a card more visually appealing, and they make a point. You might also want to design your own logo, but keep in mind this can get expensive when doing print jobs.

Can you print your cards at home? Yes. Should you? I don't think so. There is an obvious difference between homemade and professionally printed cards. We're talking twenty dollars for five hundred professionally printed cards. Don't be cheap. Spend the money.

So now you have your hundreds of business cards. What do you do with them? Give them to every client and every prospect. Give them to every contact. Take them with you to Rotary meetings and Chamber of Commerce meetings and fund-raisers. Put them inside business-related holiday cards. Take them on vacation with you. Carry them in your purse—*always*.

Which brings us to another question. What do you do with the cards that other people give you? If you don't like someone and don't care to call her ever again, throw her card away. If you think there's a remote chance you'll need to be in contact with someone again, then of course keep the card. There are any number of ways to store these. Some people—men—store them in a drawer bundled in a rubber band in no particular order. There are better ways. There are business card files you can keep on your desk that keep cards either in alphabetical order or in category order, such as vendors in one category, and service providers in another. I know people who keep cards in both orders and request two cards for that reason. That way they can find a card whether they remember the person's name or just the product or service she offers.

Stationery stores sell business card portfolios. They come in leather and in plastic. They have clear sleeves three to a page into which you insert cards. This works for a while. When your network is into the hundreds, this becomes a cumbersome way to locate someone's card.

You can also store this information on your computer. There are products that scan cards into a database and then you can access the information based on any number of factors—name, location, product. You can also input the necessary information into your computer manually or have someone else do it. The point is, if you make a contact and don't retain the information, you've lost that person as part of your network.

Announcements

Now, how do you maintain your network? That is where the other kinds of cards come in. One is announcements. Anytime anything changes about your business, send an announcement to everyone in your network. Your network includes both business contacts and personal contacts, because your next-door neighbor may well know someone who can use your services someday. Send announcements anytime your address changes or you add a staff member. Send announcements when you get a new credential: "Barbara Wilson Associates is pleased to announce that Ms. Wilson has been named to the American Academy of Froofroo Fluffers. We look forward to discussing your Froofroo Fluffing needs in the future." The announcement will include an address and phone number and other important information, and a business card or two tucked into the envelope is a good idea, as well.

Holiday Cards

I maintain my network on my home computer. I have an ever-changing list of about four hundred people. Every year I add between fifty and a hundred new people to my network and I lose about the same number. I send four hundred holiday cards every December. Is it expensive to send four hundred holiday cards? Yes, it is. Counting postage, it costs about a dollar a card. But even if I had twice as many people in my network it would still be a good investment to keep in touch. There is no point of diminishing returns when it comes to sending holiday cards. Send them to as many people as you can fairly consider in your network. But don't bother sending a card to someone you met once a year ago and never followed up with. She won't appreciate the card because she won't know who sent it.

Just to Say Thank You

The most important kind of card to send is the thank you card. When is it appropriate to send a thank you card? When is it not? People do nice things for you all the time. Send a thank you card. Some snotty teenager wrote a letter to Dear Abby saying, "If people do nice things for me it is because they want to and not because they expect to be thanked." That girl will not go far. Of course we only do nice things because we want to, but we all want to feel that our little bit of extra work or money or hospitality is appreciated. I do a lot for a lot of people. Most women do. If I buy a gift for someone I try to find "just the right gift." I don't just walk into Wal-Mart and buy a salad spinner because it's on sale, unless I know the person I am buying for enjoys salads and might like a spinner. I shop for people all year. If I see just the right necklace that I know my friend Carol will love, I buy it and keep it until her birthday or Christmas. It is not easy keeping track of people's special days and buying just the right thing. In fact, sometimes I might miss the mark, but not for lack of trying. I expect people to appreciate and acknowledge my gifts. If I send you a pound of your favorite coffee at Christmastime, I expect you to let me know you received it. I hate worrying whether my carefully planned gifts were lost in the mail, and in fact, it embarrasses me to have to call and ask, "Did my package get there?" It should embarrass the recipient even more that she did not acknowledge the gift. Keep thank you notes on hand and USE THEM.

Of course I give gifts because I want to, and to let the giftees know that they are important in my life, and therefore worthy of my gifts. However, never underestimate the power of a great thank you. My friend's mother had a seventieth birthday and I was invited to the party. This woman has everything, and I mean everything, but she appreciates nice things. I noticed once when we were out to dinner that she didn't have a purse mirror, and so for her birthday I bought her a sterling silver purse mirror and I had her monogram engraved on it. She sent me the most beautiful thank you letter. She thanked me for coming to the party and she said what a great time she had at her own party. She thanked me for the "beautiful" purse mirror and for the extra thoughtfulness of having it monogrammed. Finally, she thanked me for the best gift of all—my friendship. I can tell you that ever since then, I try to make every gift to this woman extra special. Why? Because I know she appreciates it.

The mother of another friend has cancer. She has been having radiation treatments that are wearing her out, and she is scared and depressed, of course. I wanted to do something to let this woman know that she is thought about in a special way. So, I made her chicken soup. This was some special chicken soup. It took me two days to make. I put a lot of love into that soup, and not just chicken and barley. Then before I delivered the soup I decided that woman does not live by soup alone, so I baked her some cake too. Actually, I dropped the first cake as I pulled it out of the oven so I had to bake her TWO cakes! When I delivered the cake and the soup, I gave my friend's mother a hug and for good measure I gave the father a hug, too. Then I forgot all about my "good deed." It felt good to have done it. A few days later I got a beautiful card from the mom thanking me for the delicious soup and cake and telling me she was almost finished with her treatments and feeling better about life. I felt so good to be appreciated that I immediately started planning other nice things to do for this woman.

I mentioned that I gave the mom a hug, and that I gave the dad a hug, too. Funny thing about hugs. It's hard to give one without getting one back. So, give hugs AND get hugs. Do nice things for people AND appreciate the nice things people do for you. You have a network so you will have people who will "be there" for you. They are more likely to be there in the future if you appreciate them being there for you NOW.

What other cards can we use to keep in touch with our networks? Well, one important way to keep in touch is to acknowledge other people's news. If someone we know is sick, we know to send a card. If a loved one dies, we send a card. If someone we know is promoted we should send a card. Birthday cards are fun ways to keep in touch.

Other Correspondence

What other news is appropriate for a card? Just about anything other than "hey, heard you're goin' to jail!" Several years ago I organized a teddy bear drive through my Rotary Club. We collected hundreds of darling bears and then delivered them to the

Plainfield, Illinois Rotary Club to be distributed to victims of a recent tornado there. Our local paper featured a picture of me surrounded by dozens of bears as we were loading up the delivery van. So many people cut out that picture and sent it to me with a card saying how great the project was. One local businessman had the picture laminated and he sent it to me in a card that said, "Wish I had thought of that! Good job!"

Burned Bridges and Damage Control

Just as you make friends, sometimes you lose them—sometimes through no fault of your own. Some people just decide not to expend any more energy on you. I have never really understood this concept, but it happens. Sometimes you will screw up. Fix the problem. Fix it fast and fix it well.

"Life is short" is a popular expression. But it's not true. *Life is long*. We live with the consequences of our actions *forever*. Don't burn bridges unless you absolutely have to. If you screw up, even if the screw-up is unintentional, make things right. Do whatever it takes. Why? What is one person lost in your network? Well, remember that you acquire the network of everyone in your network. You can also lose whole chunks of your own network by losing just one member of it. When someone leaves your network, she takes her network with her, for the most part. People talk. People want to associate with people who do the right thing. So do the right thing. It may be expensive or embarrassing in the short run, but not fixing your mistakes will be far more costly in the long run. Sometimes it takes time to be allowed to fix broken relationships. Sometimes you just have to sit out your penance, but usually people will accept an outstretched olive branch, and they will give you another chance.

What Is Your NET Worth?

Imagine you are a circus act. Pick your favorite . . . a high-wire walker, a trapeze artist, a human cannonball. You'd want a net. What kind of net would be good enough? Would you want a paper net or a plastic net? How about super-duper reinforced gauge intertwining net? A paper net might be the equivalent of having a single person standing under you as you performed your act. "I'll catch you," your "net" calls out. Well, she's better than no net at all. A plastic net might be two people holding a blanket between them. "We'll catch you," they assure you. And maybe they will. Think of the super-net as a crowd of supporters all standing around a circular canvas, each holding up a part. The more supporters there are, the bigger the canvas they can hold and the more likely they will truly catch you if you fall. Build the biggest, strongest, cleverest, and most loving network that you can. With a network like that, any woman can soar, safe in the knowledge that she is truly supported.

A network, after all, is your personal support system. If your net works, you will feel supported and be supported. You will have people to call when you need company and people who will understand when you need your space. You will have business contacts and employment contacts and a social circle. You will have resources when you need your questions answered. You will have the opportunity to be mentored.

You will also be a part of many other people's networks. People will be calling you for advice and for assistance. You will be respected as a leader in your community. You will have the opportunity to be a mentor!

You already have a network, of course. It starts with your family and friends and neighbors and coworkers and spreads with a little work from there. You network is in flux. You have to tend and cull your network . . . always adding, sometimes subtracting a pair of hands holding up your net. People need you and you need people. People WANT to help you. Let them. Ask for help. You know how good you feel when someone asks for your help and you are able to give it. Make other people feel good by letting them help you. Seek them out. Reach out to people who might need you but be afraid to ask.

If you already know everything and can do everything, then maybe you don't need a net. I haven't met you. Everyone I know needs one. Reach out. Be part of someone else's net. Invite someone to be part of yours.

9

Name-Dropping for Profit

(ADVANCED NETWORKING)

I told you that you acquire the network of everyone in your network. Did you know that you also can acquire the networks of people who are total and complete strangers to you? Fun, huh?

Of course you know that you can drop the name of a friend. You can drop the name of your boss. You can drop the name of your neighbor, and you can drop the name of your fellow Kiwanian. Why would you want to? Dropping names introduces an element of accountability into a conversation. If you call a lawyer to whom I refer a lot of business and drop my name, he will drop everything to help you. Why? Because he wants you to say good things about him to me so I will send him even more business.

How to Drop A Name

You know how to drop your keys, and you know how to drop a hint. How do you drop a name? Well, you do it right off, as part of your introduction. "Hi, my name is Kelly Jones. I got your name from Sarah Adams." You can be more specific if you have more specifics to give. Of course, it's a required element of the name-dropping concept that the person whose name you are dropping must be known to the person to whom you are dropping the name. Remember that "I got your name from Gina, the sister of the girl who washes your hair" is not as effective as "Your boss, Kerry, said you could help me."

Why Drop a Name?

Why drop a name? Hey, we're all busy. I am especially busy. When a stranger calls me at my office for free legal advice, I might say, "I'm sorry we don't do those kinds of cases." A smart caller will ask, "Well, do you know someone who does?" If I am in the mood to, and I know someone who does the kind of legal work she is looking for, I will give her a name, and sometimes a phone number, too. For example, I don't do divorces. If someone calls me and asks for divorce advice I will tell her, "I don't do divorces." But I know someone who does. If she asks me, I will give her the name of the best divorce lawyer I know. And if she's really smart, she'll call her up and say, "Hi, I got your name from Margaret."

If you called me and I was busy and I never heard of you, I might not take your call. But if you were referred to me by an existing client of mine—or another lawyer or my next-door neighbor—then I'll make time for you. Why? Because, I appreciate that my existing client thought of me highly enough to refer a friend in need to me. I want my existing client to continue to send me potential new clients. I want this stranger to call my client and say, "Well, she doesn't do cases like mine, but she was very helpful on the phone, and she explained how I could get help." I never want anyone to call someone in my network and say, "She didn't take my call," or "She was no help at all." So, if you have a name to drop, drop it. Do it right up front.

What Can You Accomplish by Dropping a Name?

You'd be surprised what a little name-dropping can do. When I was in college, I did an internship in the office of my state senator. Whenever a constituent had a problem that she couldn't solve on her own, I would make a phone call to see what could be done. Of course, every conversation started with, "Hello, I'm calling from Senator A's office and one of our constituents needs help." Dropping Senator A's name got all kinds of action.

If I was calling a state agency, then, of course, the agency would be thinking about next year's budget and would want to make sure the senator would support an increase. If I was calling a local business, the business might be thinking it would like to have a traffic light installed at its intersection someday, and need the senator's help. The possibilities are endless. When my internship was over, I had to write a paper. I wrote that the single most impressive thing about working for a senator is being able to drop his name to accomplish things I probably couldn't have accomplished otherwise. It was empowering—especially to an eighteen-year-old kid.

Now I am a lawyer and I can drop my OWN name. "This is *Attorney* Margaret Basch calling" gets almost as much mileage as "Senator A's office." If you did not go to law school, don't worry. There are plenty of names for you to drop.

You can drop the name of anyone in your network. If you're lucky, you can even get an introduction. When I refer a client to another lawyer—or to my accountant or my doctor—I always call ahead and say, "Take care of my client." This is the ideal way to make a contact.

I have a dear friend who graduated from Harvard Law School. He told me a story about being on *Law Review* there. If you were on *Law Review* at Harvard, the faculty advisor of the publication would call up a Supreme Court justice, and say, 'Your Honor, have I got a law clerk for *you*!" The justice would be happy and the Harvard grad would get a job as a clerk at the Supreme Court. Then, at the end of two years, that same Supreme Court justice would call the managing partner of World's Most Prestigious Law Firm and say, "Have I got an associate for you." The firm would be happy to get a call from a Supreme Court justice with a recommendation, and, of course, the Harvard grad/law clerk would get a great job with a wonderful law firm. The world is not perfect, though, and this doesn't always happen for the rest of us. That's okay. Since you have acquired the network of everyone in your network, you can call and make your own introduction with confidence.

I told you you can acquire the networks of people not in your network. Perfect strangers can provide names to drop, although this is a little trickier. Let me give you my favorite story of name-dropping (of course, the names I dropped have been changed here). It is my favorite because it's a multi-level drop. There was a charity I suspected of being bogus. I *hate* bogus charities. I did some research on this charity and I found out that it consistently brought in millions of dollars every year. Of course, because it's a charity, all of those millions of dollars in donations were deducted on lots of people's taxes, which means that you and I were subsidizing this charity. The charity's stated purpose was to help children with cancer. Who doesn't want to help children with cancer?

When I read the statements that this charity filed with the appropriate state office, I saw that the charity spent *all* the money it brought in on itself. It paid its several employees hundreds of thousands of dollars a year in salaries. The employees traveled all over the country, first class. The board members were flown in for meetings, first class. Yet, the two lines on this charity's statements—"How much did you give for aid to individuals?" and "How much did you give for grants to foundations?"—were both *zero* for every year this charity was in existence. I could maybe understand that for the first year or two, when a charity is starting up, most of the money donated would have to be spent on administrative costs, but after a number of years, the start-up should be complete and some, if not most, of the money should go to the cause.

I called the Charities Department of the state involved; it wasn't Colorado, but let's say it was. I said, "Hi, I ordered these statements, and now I have them, and this charity spends all of its millions of dollars in donations on salaries and first-class travel." The bureaucrat said, "Do you know how many charities we have in Colorado? We can't monitor them all." Well, I can understand that they can't do more than a perfunctory read of the statements as they come in, but I had read the things. I was telling them, "*Look!* A bogus charity!" Apparently they didn't care, or they didn't have a system in place to deal with bogus charities. I wondered why they bothered collecting these statements at all, but if they didn't, I wouldn't have been able to acquire the information.

My first inclination was to forget the notion of busting the bogus charity. I figured if the government didn't care, why should I care? What could I do? I lamented that all those people were giving all that money thinking they were helping sick kids, but I figured "Hey, they could order these reports, just like I did, if they really cared." Well, maybe I just care too much about sick kids, or maybe I was thinking about all the good those millions of dollars could do if they were going to real charities. Or maybe the thought of those mopes eating caviar in first class was more than I could bear, but I couldn't let it go.

Finally, I mentioned it to a friend of mine from law school whom I'll call Giorgio. Luckily, he was as outraged as I, and luckily, he is an Assistant United States Attorney, here in Chicago. He tried to help me directly, but his office would not pursue a case in another state. So he told me, "I took a class with Ann Jones, an Assistant U.S. Attorney from Boulder. Call her." So I called Ann Jones; the first thing I said to her was, "Hi, I'm a friend of Giorgio, from the U.S. Attorney's office in Chicago." Ann remembered him. I told her the story about the charity, and I told her Giorgio said she might be able to help me. This was step one in the name-dropping process. I had acquired the network of someone in my network.

The next step was more impressive in terms of name-dropping. Ann didn't care to help me, or was too busy to, but she didn't want me to go back to Giorgio empty-handed. After all, he was in her network and she might need help from a U.S. Attorney in Chicago someday. So she said, "You know, that sounds like something the Postal Inspection Service in Boulder would handle as a charity fraud case. Why don't you call there?" I was a little disappointed and wondered whether I was getting the run-around. When I called, I told the receptionist I was calling about a suspected case of charity fraud. She referred me back to the state's Department of Charities. So I said, "Ann Jones of the U.S. Attorney's office told me you would help me."

I heard a pause on the phone line, and then the receptionist said, "I'll connect you with Inspector Kielbasa. He's the team leader for the fraud division." So by dropping the name of a complete stranger, I was able to get into a network that otherwise would have been closed to me. Should life work like this? Shouldn't the government help everyone who needs help and not just those who have a name to drop? Of course. Is the real world a perfect world? Not on your life. The better your network and the more adept you are at name-dropping, the more pleasant and efficient your world can become.

My sister, who drops my name more often than cruise ships drop anchor, put herself in a bind. Back in the old days, you had to buy a house within two years of the sale of your residence house or you had to pay the capital gains tax. My sister sold her house in the suburbs and then thought it would be daring to live in the city for a couple years. She did, and I'm sure she had a blast, but she waited until the very last minute to look for a house to buy within the two-year period following the sale of her first house. If she did not close the purchase in time, she would have to pay thousands of dollars in capital gains taxes. So she found a house and she signed a contract and she applied for a mortgage.

The mortgage bank knew of my sister's time constraints. They had a copy of the contract that stated the closing date. She even asked the mortgage officer if closing on that date would be a problem, and she explained the time constraints. "Oh, no problem," she was told. As her free lawyer, I had contact with the bank over the course of the two months between signing and closing. They assured me over and over again that closing on time would not be a problem. Every time they asked for a document or additional information, my sister ran out and got it for them in an expedient manner. Nobody was worried until the Friday before the Tuesday closing. The manager of the mortgage department called me and said, "We're not going to get it done." Just like that. She didn't even say "sorry." She didn't have an excuse. She just said, "We're busy." I went ballistic, which I don't do often. (No sane person wants to be on the receiving end of me when I'm ballistic.) I was actually screaming at the woman, which she didn't appreciate, but ask me if I cared. I yelled, "You knew she had to close by this date. You assured her there was no problem. You've had every document you needed from her for more than a month. And now, three days before the closing, you're telling me you're not going to get it done?!" "Yeppers."

I wracked my brain to figure how to crack the bank's hierarchy. I was already dealing with the manager of the mortgage department, and she wouldn't let me talk to anyone else—I asked. I thought about calling the president of my bank and asking if he knew the president of this podunk bank, but I doubted he would (and I didn't know the president of my bank anyway). Then I remembered that a member of the Rotary Club in the town where that bank is located visited my Rotary Club once, and we met. I looked up his number in the Rotary District Directory and I called him. If he didn't remember me, he didn't say so. I explained that I needed a contact at the bank in his town and I asked him if he knew anyone there. Well, he said, the president of that bank used to be a member of Rotary. His name was Joe Cooper. I called Mr. Cooper and I left a voice mail message.

"Hello, Mr. Cooper," I said. "My name is Margaret and I am having a problem with your bank. My friend Jeff Rotarian suggested you might be able to help me." Then I explained the situation. After a not-too-pleasant hour of panicking, I got a phone call. It was that nice lady mortgage manager at the bank. They were going to be able to get the paperwork done in time for my sister to close on Tuesday after all. Ta-da.

What if you just don't have any name to drop at all? What if no one in your network knows anyone in the network you need to tap into? It happens sometimes, although, the bigger and stronger your own network is, the more likely you know someone who knows THE someone who can help you.

I was telling another lawyer about this chapter. His initial reaction was, "Name-dropping is a chapter?" I happen to know that this lawyer is an expert name-dropper. His father is a prominent lawyer in town, and they both belong to the same private club. Men name-drop because they know it works. They are adept at it. It is a skill they pass on from father to son. Women are more reluctant to name-drop, but they shouldn't be. If someone refers you to me it is an HONOR. It means the person doing the referring thinks highly of me. If you call me and say, "Sadie Brown said you might be able to help me," I hear, "Sadie Brown thinks highly of you. She respects you and she trusts you with her friends' problems." It is good to be a name-dropper. It is good to be a name-droppee. And it is also good to be the name dropped. It creates a warm, fuzzy feeling all the way around.

My lawyer friend told me a story about a client of his who makes pool tables. His lifelong desire was to sell his pool tables through a particular national chain of retail stores. He tried to make a contact within the purchasing department of the chain, with no success. National chains get solicited on a huge scale. The man scoured his network for a contact at this national chain. Finally, he had an idea. He called the purchasing department, and instead of asking them to buy his products, he asked for the name of a manufacturer's representative that they could recommend. They recommended one, and, of course, it was one with which the chain does business.

The pool table maker called the recommended manufacturer's representative, and what did he do? He dropped a name. "Hi, I got your name from the purchasing department at National Retail Chain. I was hoping you could help me." As you might imagine, this resourceful name-dropper now successfully distributes his pool tables to the manufacturer's rep who sells them to the national chain, which markets them to the public. So if you think creatively, you can usually come up with a way to get a droppable name from a stranger.

Dropping Names in the Workplace

I have never worked for a big corporation or in a small cubicle. Most Americans are not so lucky. I drop names to get business and to get things done, mostly to avoid filing lawsuits. However, name-dropping does have a place in the corporate setting.

Consider an example my brother shared. While working as a financial analyst at a huge corporation, he was given a project by the president of the company. My brother needed to supply the analysis and answers to the president later that same day. Of course, the pressure was on, because my brother wanted to shine in the president's eyes.

Some of the data my brother needed in order to complete his analysis was not within his knowledge. He needed to depend on others within the corporation to provide facts and figures. So what did he do?

He called another employee of the company and he asked for the required information. He did not, however, just say, "Hi, this is Rick, and I am working on a project." As my brother put it, in a corporate setting, who *isn't* working on a project? Rick said, "This is Rick and I am working on a project for Joe Bigshoes (otherwise known as president of the company), and I need this information today."

What he didn't say is as important as what he did say. He didn't say, "If you don't get me this information today, I'll report to President Bigshoes that I couldn't finish the project because you dropped the ball. If I go down, I take you with me." But he might as well have. If you aren't important in the corporate scheme of things, but your boss or your department *is*, and you're working on an especially important project, then say so. People are more willing to stick their necks out if they know that they'll be held accountable. After all, the next names you drop might be theirs, and especially if you know important people, they want you to say only the best possible things about them. Voilà. Help.

Name-Dropping in the Job Search

I've never really had to seek out a job. Thank goodness, because it doesn't sound like fun. I got a job right out of law school and then I got hired away from that job by another firm. When I left the firm, I struck out on my own. So many of my friends, especially older women, seem to be losing their jobs of long standing, and they're having a hard time landing in the marketplace. One of them, Laura, shared her name-dropping story with me.

Laura was out of work for a year. She didn't mind at first. She considered unemployment an unexpected but welcome extended vacation. Then her savings started running low, and she got serious about her job search. Because she had built a tremendous network while she was working—participating in women's groups within her chosen profession—she had lots of people to call and lots of names to drop. People she knew, she called. People she didn't know personally, she name-dropped. She would write a letter and say, "I met Katie Kelley at the NATWR meeting last year and I was impressed that she talked about how wonderful Successful Employer, Inc. is. Now that I am back in the market, I would be interested in pursuing opportunities there."

If you are searching for a job, call everyone you know. If they can't help, get more names, and then DROP them!

One Name Dropped Can Snowball into an Avalanche of Helpful Names

The idea for this book came from an editor friend. I told her, "I've always said that every woman should go to law school, even if she never intends to practice law. No one can ever take away that education."

She said, "You should write a book, and you should call it *Every Woman Should Go to Law School or Read This Book*, and you should teach women all those things that you have learned to help them get ahead." She also gave me the name of an editor at a publisher she thought might be interested.

That person gave me the name of a woman who, as it turned out, was looking for books for women. In the meantime, I had written a proposal for this book. I sent the proposal to the new editor, and next thing I knew, she was calling me to make an offer on it!

The same woman who had the idea for this book became a name to drop. Then, through a series of dropped names, this book became a reality.

Name-Dropping Is a Two-Way Street

I don't mind helping out your friends when they have legal problems. Any friend of yours is a friend of mine, as they say. I will, however, expect that if you send me your friends who need free legal advice or minor legal work, that you'll *also* send me your next-door neighbor when she gets run over by a truck. Don't send me the crud and then send the good stuff to someone else. I won't appreciate that, and neither will anyone else when you do it to them.

I will sometimes have a client call my accountant when she

needs a quick answer to a tax question. My accountant will help out because my client dropped my name. I'll also recommend my accountant when someone needs to hire one to do tax work or bookkeeping. It's a two-way street. He helps my people who need help because he knows I also send him people who do HIM some benefit.

If you're lucky enough to have people in your network refer business or contacts to you, appreciate the effort. Do the best possible job for the referred person or business, and thank the referrer for the contact. Believe it or not, I have referred business to other lawyers and gotten bad reports back. I never send anyone to these lawyers again. If I refer someone to a lawyer and that lawyer can't help my friend or client, I expect the lawyer to at least treat the person nicely, and maybe recommend someone else. If my friend is overcharged or neglected by a lawyer or other person in my network, I'll hear about it. I value everyone in my network and I want my people treated right. I have a large network, and if one person in my network will not help someone else in my network, I'll find someone else who will. Not only will I send my friends who need a favor, I'll send my friends who have big, high-paying contracts. Keep that in mind when a friend sends someone to you for help.

Name-Dropping for Fun

Sometimes you can drop a name for fun instead of for profit. When there's something you want but don't know how to get, name-dropping can help. My sister and I went to a famous pop singer's concert in Las Vegas. The maitre'd gave us crummy seats. While we were sitting in the boondocks, I mentioned to my sister that I once did some legal work for the singer's father. My sister said, "Oh, you should send him a note." I said, "He won't care that I did work for his father," and my sister said, "So? What do you have to lose?"

So I wrote a little note on the back of my business card and sent it backstage. I really did not expect any favor for it, but as it turned out, just before the concert started, the maitre'd came and got my sister and me and moved us up to the front of the crowd, right by the stage. It was a nice gesture by the singer.

One of the other people now in my network is the guy who spits out the tickets at a Chicago sports arena. He just happened to give my sister and me great seats at a game once. He was a stranger to us, but we remembered his name, and as we were leaving the game we stopped and thanked him for the upgrade. Every time we go to that stadium again, we go looking for "Bob" and he always upgrades us, just because we look for him. He doesn't really know us. If he's not around, we usually say to the other ticket agent, "Gee, do you know where Bob is?" The agent's seen us with Bob, and we're using his name, so he assumes we're "friends of Bob's" and upgrades us, too. I'm not sure how Bob became part of our network exactly, except that we appreciate the one favor he did us, and we certainly appreciate him now.

Tread Carefully

There are times when it's not appropriate to drop a name. Some people in our society are supposed to be impartial. We pay them to be impartial. Don't insult their impartiality. I'm referring to people like judges and police officers, health inspectors and hearing officers.

It's not a good idea, if you are pulled over for speeding, to tell the officer that you'll report his conduct to his chief at Rotary tomorrow. No one is above the law, so take the ticket. If you really believe you're not guilty, then go to court and make your case.

Don't go to court and tell the judge that you're friends with his boss, the chief judge. Trying to intimidate a judge is the same as trying to bribe one. A judge friend told me he denied a lawyer's motion once and the lawyer had the nerve to say, "Oh, but I'm friends with Judge X (the presiding judge of the Circuit Court of Cook County)." My judge friend was outraged, as well he should have been. It also didn't do a thing to change the denied motion.

Drop names when you can benefit yourself, but do it judiciously. Don't threaten people. Don't try to get away with something you know darn well you shouldn't get away with. Your friends are your friends, and they will help you when they can. Don't abuse that friendship by asking more of your friends than is reasonable or right.

10

An Embarrassment of Resources

(MORE PLACES AND WAYS TO FIND THE HELP YOU NEED)

We have our networks of family and friends and neighbors and associates and professionals. We are supported by the people who care about us. Where else can we turn when we are feeling overwhelmed? What if we are sick and have no insurance? What if we need a lawyer and can't afford one? What if we're just at the ends of our ropes? Well, there's a whole support system you might not know about.

Sometimes strangers are better than friends when it comes to seeking help. Sometimes we're embarrassed to tell our friends and families that we're feeling depressed or that we've been sued or any number of problems. Psychologists get rich listening to people who would rather talk to a stranger than a friend. In the final analysis, your network is your greatest asset as you maneuver through life. Even if your network can't help solve your problem, there *is* a solution.

Physical Health

If Mama's sick, ain't nobody happy. When I have a headache, all I can think is "I have a headache." I have similar thoughts for backaches and stomachaches. It's hard to be productive when we're sick.

When very bad things happen to people, when they go bankrupt or when they lose their jobs or they come home to find their house burned to the ground, they always say, "Well, at least we have our health." Health is more important than money. Just ask a rich person with an incurable illness if she would trade all her money for good health.

Many women don't have health insurance. Some women work two or three jobs and still don't have health insurance—for themselves OR their children. It's a luxury some women can't afford. So what happens when they get sick? Do they have to forego medical care and hope for the best? No. Every hospital emergency room and acute care center in the country will treat someone in distress. If you break a bone, an emergency room doctor will set it. If you have chest pains, no hospital will turn you away. If your kid falls off the jungle gym and cuts her knee open, an emergency room will stitch it up, whether you have insurance or not.

Don't avoid getting care because you don't have insurance. After an emergency room treats you, they might set you up with a staff social worker who will determine if you are eligible for assistance from any number of programs. You also might be eligible for Medicaid if you meet certain financial restrictions.

What if you get sick because of an illness they don't treat in emergency rooms, like cancer or AIDS or hepatitis or lupus? No quick fix in the ER is going to make things right. How do you get long-term care?

Too many women don't get mammograms or pelvic exams because they think they can't afford to. "What if they find something?" they reason, "How could I afford care?" I'm telling you that every woman and every kid can get medical care. You might have to do some legwork and find the right resources for you, but they are there.

I had a friend who found a breast lump. She had just started a new job after having been out of work for quite a long time. She had no health insurance. Her sister had died of breast cancer the year before. She was beside herself. A relatively young woman, she was already planning how she would tell her parents about her death sentence.

My friend turned to the medical clinic of a major teaching hospital in Chicago. It turned out she did have cancer. The mammography and subsequent testing were free to my friend because she met the clinic's financial eligibility requirements. The subsequent mastectomy, chemotherapy, radiation, and all her prescription anti-nausea medications were also free. When she began to feel overwhelmed (her family lived several hundred miles away *and* she lost her new job because she had to miss so much time), the clinic provided her access to psychiatric help and prescription anti-depressants. I'm happy to report that my friend is now doing fine. She has since moved closer to her family and started a new job there. She's happy and optimistic about her condition.

There are so many resources for medical care that it's impossible to list them all. Hospitals and medical schools have clinics. The federal government and other sources often award grants and subsidies for the care of people who would not otherwise have access to medical treatment. If you go to a medical school clinic or a teaching hospital, you will get much of your attention from medical students and interns. However, they're all under the direct supervision of a teaching doctor. Teaching hospitals and medical schools give notoriously good care. Dental schools have clinics, too, where you can get inexpensive dental care, performed by advanced dental students under the supervision of a dentist/ professor. If your local community college has a dental hygiene program, check there about getting inexpensive cleanings and exams.

Another place to go for free medical care is a county hospital. Large metropolitan areas all have county hospitals that get federal and local government subsidies to provide medical care to those who could not otherwise afford treatment. They don't turn anyone away.

Many communities have routine care available to residents in need. My local area has a program called Access to Care. Each community in the area contributes money to the program and they have a list of doctors who are willing to see patients referred by Access to Care. This might be a good way to get your mammogram or for you to get your kids immunized.

All communities have a health department and many of them have a senior center or senior coordinator. These are good sources of information about health resources in your community. Some towns have a visiting nurse who will look in on the elderly at no cost to you. They can perform routine tasks like filling prescription boxes and taking blood pressure. If you don't know all the health resources in your town, call city hall and find out. Don't make yourself sick worrying about getting sick. Get care.

Mental Health

It's normal to sometimes feel overwhelmed, sad, and worried. But sometimes these feelings last longer than they should, and they start to control our lives. How do we deal with these funks? We can yell at our kids, stuff our faces, or stay home with the curtains closed and the phone off the hook. Better yet, we can get help.

Mental health resources are everywhere. If you need to talk to someone, or if you need psychiatric care, you can get help. There are public mental health centers in every community. These centers are funded by tax dollars and they usually do private fundraising as well. Sometimes they get grants from foundations. Sometimes they throw fashion shows or dances to make money. They do these things so they can afford to provide mental health resources to everyone who needs them. Usually they provide their services on a sliding scale, so you pay what you can afford. If you can't afford to pay anything, they'll see you anyway.

Because many of my clients have lost children in tragic accidents or they've been crippled themselves and are in constant pain, I sometimes refer them to our local mental health clinic. Some of these people would never think of reaching out for help, and the fact that I refer them gives legitimacy to getting mental help.

Sometimes our burdens are too heavy to bear without help. Mental health care is not just for the mentally ill. It is also for the mentally anguished. There is no sitgma attached to it. Please, if you or someone you care about is feeling overwhelmed, GET HELP.

Why Do You Think They Call It Insurance?

So many calls to my office are from worried people who have been sued or are about to be. I always ask if they have appropriate insurance, and if they do, I tell them to call their insurance agent. Every home owner who has a mortgage has home owner's insurance. The mortgage holder requires it. Why is home owner's insurance so important? Two reasons. It protects your house and all its contents so that you won't be left homeless or without the necessities or luxuries of life. This is called property coverage. It also protects you when you injure someone or damage someone else's property. This is called liability coverage. Why does home owner's insurance cover you when you injure someone else? Because if the injured party took a judgment against you, they could put a lien on your house and you could lose it.

When I use the term home owner's insurance, I'm including in this category renter's insurance and condominium owner's insurance. Basically they're the same—they include property coverage and liability coverage. Condo insurance doesn't cover outside walls because the association's insurance covers those. Renter's insurance doesn't include any part of the building; it only covers the contents. These are the only differences.

So when does property coverage kick in? I took a course in insurance in law school, and I still don't know everything there is to know. I recently called my insurance agent, and he didn't know the answers to my questions, either. He was even somewhat taken aback that I assumed he'd know what was covered on my home owner's policy. "Those are claims questions," he told me. The only way to know what's covered on your insurance is to read the policy. Yes, I do understand that this is a daunting task.

Insurance companies all have brochures which "explain" the coverage. I read a stack of them. They make it sound like you are covered for every possible loss. You aren't. You're only covered for the losses specifically listed in your policy. Just because you're covered for fire, theft, vandalism, wind, rain, sleet, and hail, doesn't mean you're covered for accidental breakage. If you want to be covered for accidental breakage, then you have to buy "all risks" insurance, which is available on an item-by-item basis.

For example, if you have a valuable antique lamp and you want to be protected in the event a guest in your home knocks it over and breaks it, then you should buy a rider to your home owner's policy specifically to insure the lamp for "all risks." The general rule for damage to property in your home is that if a vandal does it, it's covered. If you do it or a guest does it, it's not covered. A columnist friend of mine calls this the Dracula principle. If you let Dracula into your home, then he is a guest and you accept responsibility for any injury he might cause there. If Dracula breaks in and does damage, on the other hand, you're covered.

On the positive side, if a guest in your home damages your lamp—or vase or carpet—then the guest's home owner's insurance should cover the damage. Does this make sense? Not really, but then insurance is pretty much a take it or leave it proposition. You can't negotiate an insurance policy. That's why courts always read policies in favor of the insured—*you*. If there's any question under a fair reading of an insurance policy whether you're covered or not, you're covered, because the insurance company drafted the contract and plainly could have drafted it in its own favor if that was its intention.

Why do so few people understand insurance? Well, the policies have a lot to do with it. Nobody takes the time to read a twenty-page, single-spaced contract until they have a claim, and even then most of us just call our agents and ask, "Is this covered?" What if he says no? Do we take his word for it? I called several lawyers and then I called my columnist friend (the one with the Dracula principle) and I asked them all the same claims question. Even my insurance agent didn't know the answer. Only the columnist answered correctly. If in doubt, check it out. Why is this so important? Because you're covered for incidents you might never have thought of, and if you don't ask, you won't receive the money that you might well have coming to you.

If your property is damaged or stolen by a third party, your insurance will repair or replace it. If a pipe breaks and your house is flooded, your property coverage will pay for the damage. If you live in a condo and a pipe breaks in your unit and the unit below yours is damaged, then your liability coverage should pay.

If you host a party in your home and in the morning you notice a sterling silver antique ladle is missing, you can make a claim on your property insurance. Your property is covered whether it's inside your home or elsewhere. If you chain your bicycle to a rack at the mall and it's stolen while you are shopping, your home owner's insurance will buy you a new one. You're covered any time your property is damaged unless you damage it yourself. If you let a friend ride your bike and your friend falls off the bike and damages it, it's as if you damaged it yourself. On the other hand, if you leave your garage door open and a neighbor kid takes your bike for a joy ride without your permission or knowledge and then trashes it, then it's covered.

Insurance can be a valuable resource when you least expect it. I had a client many years ago who was crossing Harrison Street in Chicago, in front of Cook County Hospital. She was in the crosswalk, and she was hit by a car. The car and driver were uninsured. So what did we do? We filed a claim on my client's automobile insurance policy. She had uninsured motorist coverage. My client was shocked that her car insurance would pay the claim. She thought—as I believe most people think—that her car insurance only covered her while she was in her car. In fact, your car insurance covers you when you are hit by a car, as well.

Every home owner knows she's covered on her home owner's

insurance when anyone is injured on her property. If the mailman falls in a hole in your driveway, turn it over to your insurance. If you have a barbecue in the backyard and a board breaks in the deck, injuring your neighbor, make a claim with your insurance. You actually have medical pay coverage that will pay the medical bills of any person injured on your property, whether or not it's your fault. This doesn't apply to you or anyone who lives in your house. If you fall out of bed in the morning, make a claim on your health insurance, not on your home owner's policy.

Many women don't know that the liability portion of their home owner's insurance "travels." If you're playing golf and you forget to yell, "Fore!" and the ball whacks another golfer, your homeowner's policy will pay for any injury the other golfer may have sustained. If your daughter hits a home run playing ball in your neighbor's yard and she breaks a window, your home owner's insurance will pay to replace it. I get a lot of calls from women saying, "So-and-so is threatening to sue me because he was injured when I . . ." I always tell them to make a claim on their home owner's insurance policy.

Property coverage also travels. If you drive your car into the city to have dinner with friends, and someone breaks into your car and steals your Mont Blanc from out of the console, your car insurance will pay for the damaged window, but your home owner's policy will pay for the replacement of the pen. Again, you're only covered for stated losses, unless you have an all-risks policy. If you simply lose the pen, you're not covered on your basic home owner's policy. If you want a pen insured against all risks, then you must buy a special rider for the pen.

Is this confusing enough for you? I thought it might be. My purpose here is to get you thinking of your insurance as a resource. Make sure you have as much insurance as you can manage. It will provide coverage for the multitude of mishaps you have thought about and sometimes you'll find you have coverage for things you never could have imagined. If you have questions about your coverage, ask your agent. Read the policy if you have to. I know—it sounds like an awful proposition even to me. Remember that if it's not listed, it's not covered. A lawyer friend of mine found out the hard way that his home owner's policy did not cover flooding. After he'd spent thousands of dollars of his own money repairing flood damage to his home and personal property, he bought a flood insurance rider to his regular policy—which did, in fact, pay the next time his home flooded.

There's a policy called "Personal Liability Umbrella." Most of my clients can barely afford basic insurance, but I mention the umbrella because it's a lot of coverage for not much money. It typically provides a million dollars of additional liability coverage for a few hundred dollars a year. If you're in a car accident and injure someone so seriously that they need ongoing care, you could be sued for hundreds of thousands of dollars. You could be stuck if your car insurance is exhausted. The same applies to home owner's insurance. If you drive a golf cart over someone's foot, and she loses the foot, you'll be glad to have an umbrella policy. Umbrella policies provide some additional coverages that aren't generally offered on other policies. For example, you might not be covered for defamation or invasion of privacy on your home owner's policy, but an umbrella policy typically would provide coverage for those kinds of claims.

Remember that you're not insured for intentional torts under any policy of insurance. If you purposely back your car over your ex-husband or the young man who impregnated your daughter, your insurance company will not pay the claim. If you throw a brick through your neighbor's picture window because the neighbors are being too loud and you have to get up early in the morning, you're not covered. Your insurance company may be obligated to provide you a defense—which means that they'll send a lawyer to court with you in the civil case against you. But if

a judge or jury finds you did damage to property or injured someone intentionally, then you're on your own. Intentional acts are
not insurable (nor would we want them to be). Remember, too,
that your insurance company's duty to defend you (and your family members who live in your house) only extends to civil cases. If
your son drives over the neighbor's lawn and damages it, the
insurance company may send a lawyer to defend your son in the
neighbor's case against him for repair of the lawn, but you and
your son are on your own in finding a lawyer to defend him in
criminal court.

Drunk driving is a hybrid. It may be considered an intentional
act, in that someone intentionally imbibed alcohol and then got
behind the wheel of a car. Insurance companies don't want to
cover drunk drivers, for obvious reasons. Most courts have held
that drunk drivers are covered under their automobile policies, at
least for injuries they cause to innocent third parties, because any
other result would leave innocent people without compensation.

If you have questions about items you think should be covered
but your insurance company refuses, you do have some options.
First, do your research. You know how to use a law library. You
can look up similar cases and see how the courts have held on
issues like yours. You can call a lawyer and get your questions
answered; see the section below on how to get free legal advice.
Sometimes your agent will go to bat for you—the agent is out in
the community selling insurance and it's good public relations to
have claims paid. If you absolutely cannot resolve your differences, most policies require you to arbitrate your claims. If your
car is burglarized and you and the company cannot agree on the
value of the missing items, you might want to arbitrate if the difference is big enough. If, on the other hand, you honestly believe
that your insurance company is acting in bad faith, then you can
contact your state's department of insurance, or you can file a lawsuit—but you'll probably need a lawyer to do that.

Taxing Experiences

Nothing is certain but death and taxes. Even people who don't owe taxes usually have to file a tax return. I took tax courses in law school and I did my own taxes for years, yet all of sudden my tax return became too complicated for me to do. So what does a woman do when she wants to do her taxes right but worries she isn't up to the job? If you have a complicated return, like I do, it's probably because you own a business, or you have some weird investments, like limited partnerships or historic properties. Then, hire someone to do your taxes unless you are a tax whiz yourself. If you have a simple return but still can't do your own taxes, you can hire any one of the numerous tax services out there, and they will probably do a credible job. So shop around.

What if you work and need to file a tax return but can't afford to pay for help? Help is all around. The American Association for Retired People (AARP) has programs all around the country to help seniors do their taxes. Many universities have student volunteers (usually accounting students, but sometimes finance or other majors) who help people with their taxes. So if you live near a university and you need help, call the university's general administration office and ask about available services.

The I.R.S. also offers help by way of a program called VITA: Volunteer Income Tax Assistance. The I.R.S. trains volunteers who work at libraries, malls, churches, and community centers all over the country on Saturdays to help people of moderate means (as opposed to low income) do their taxes. As of this writing, moderate is judged to be somewhere in the vicinity of $30,000 a year for an individual, which beats the very low income restrictions for some other help programs. VITA helps with federal and state returns, and even offers electronic filing for free, so you can get your refund faster if you are owed one. More information about VITA is available at the I.R.S. web site: www.irs.ustreas.gov.

Talk Is Cheap, Until You Talk to a Lawyer (Or Is It?)

You need a lawyer. You know you do. You've been sued, or you need to sue someone. You've got the government on your back. Your underage kid got busted at a party drinking liquor. You're being stalked by a crazed ex-boyfriend. Your husband died. He didn't have a big estate, but you need to transfer some stocks into your own name. Lawyers can be so darn expensive! What do you do if you really need a lawyer and you really can't afford one?

If you've been sued, consider the insurance alternative first. Are you covered for the claim? Does your insurance company owe you a defense? If so, turn over the claim, and let your insurance company hire a lawyer to represent you. Don't worry that the insurance company will hire you an under-qualified lawyer. Insurance companies have lots of lawyers both on staff and on retainer who have experience handling claims just like yours.

If you get served with papers—a summons and complaint—because you were involved in a car accident, or because your dog bit a salesman, or because your mother's cousin's son fell off your deck last Labor Day, turn the claim over to your insurance company and let them handle it. Sometimes your first clue that you're about to be sued is a Notice Of Attorney's Lien. This is a document telling you that a lawyer is representing a person who may have a claim against you. If you turn it over to your insurance company right away, the company might be able to settle any claims and avoid a lawsuit. If you throw the papers in the garbage, you're almost guaranteed to be a defendant in civil court.

Contingency Cases

What if you're a civil plaintiff and you just can't do it yourself? The plaintiff is the one doing the suing. What if you're the one who was bit by the dog or who slipped and fell on someone else's property? In personal injury cases you can almost always get an attorney on a contingent fee basis. Contingent fees mean the lawyer gets a percentage of the settlement or award that you eventually receive. Usually this amount is one-third, but it can vary. In contingent fee cases, the lawyer receives no fee unless you win your case. It's important to understand, though, that costs of litigation are figured separately from the fee. The costs of filing a complaint, servicing the summons, ordering medical records, court reporters, and the like, all come out of the settlement. So, if you settle your case for $21,000, your lawyer would get $7,000 (assuming a one-third contingency), and then the lawyer would be reimbursed for the expenses advanced by her (say $500), then you would get what's left; in this case, $13,500.

The good thing about contingent fees, of course, is that if there is no award, there is no fee. Keep in mind, though, that under the rules of professional conduct, you are responsible for the costs, win or lose. Lawyers are not allowed to lend money to clients, except for advancing the costs of pursuing your case. The costs are *always* the client's responsibility—win or lose. I've never heard of a lawyer suing a client for the expenses of a case the lawyer lost, but it could happen. So, tread carefully.

Keep in mind, too, that you may end up paying your lawyer far more on a contingency case than you would if the same lawyer handled the same case on an hourly basis. If you hire me to do your car accident case, and I spend three hours on it and I make six thousand dollars, then I've made two thousand dollars an hour. That is far more than the going rate for even the best hourly attorneys. On the other hand, I'm assuming all the risks of your litigation that an hourly attorney avoids. You always have the option of hiring a lawyer on an hourly basis instead of a contingent fee, even in a car accident case, but it never happens. Clients don't like to take risks, and most people don't budget for legal assistance. They couldn't retain a lawyer on an hourly basis, even if they wanted to.

Contingent fees are only available in personal injury cases and in other very rare litigation matters. When the possibility of a very large award exists in a non–personal injury case, sometimes lawyers will take a contingent fee, but usually not. Usually, if you want to sue or have been sued, you'll have to pay your lawyer by the hour. So, if you are about to enter into the legal system in an adversarial situation, how do you get the help you need?

Pro Bono Publico

Lawyers are not required to do charity work, but all of us do. Sometimes we volunteer on boards of charities. Sometimes we man the *pro se* desk at the courthouse. Sometimes we take cases that are referred to us by any number of advocacy groups in the community. You'll find that lawyers who are interested in civil rights issues will take cases for free that involve issues like freedom of speech and freedom of religion. A person who's persecuted or treated unfairly can very often not afford to hire a lawyer. The American Civil Liberties Union (ACLU) is an example of an advocacy group for which many attorneys volunteer. The Anti-Defamation League helps Jewish people who are discriminated against. Battered women's groups around the country have attorney volunteers who help battered women in court. Sometimes they help them get orders of protection, to keep abusive partners away. Sometimes they help women get divorces that they might not otherwise be able to afford. Students in universities often have access to free legal assistance from Student Legal Services offices.

Many metropolitan areas have a group of lawyers interested in promoting the arts. In Chicago, the Lawyers for the Creative Arts can help a theater group file incorporation papers or help an individual artist file a claim against an art gallery. Again, these lawyers are all volunteering their time.

There's a different kind of volunteering that lawyers do. We get on lists to provide free legal assistance to people who have been prescreened according to financial need. I do a case or two a year for Chicago Volunteer Legal Services (CVLS). It's impossible to tell you all the myriad services volunteer lawyers provide to people in need.

There's also a national network of government-funded or partially government-funded Legal Aid bureaus. They can be found all over the country. Some are city-wide and some in rural areas are regional. Legal Assistance Foundation of Chicago and Cook County Legal Assistance Foundation are two in Chicago. They both get grants and also do private fund-raising to support their efforts to provide legal aid to people who can't afford to hire a private lawyer.

The problem with Legal Aid is their income requirements. Not only must you not be able to afford a lawyer, you can't be able to afford anything else. As of this writing, an individual (single-person household) must gross less than $12,000 a year to qualify for help from Legal Aid.

There may be too many attorneys in this country, but there are not too many lawyers representing working people. I've spent days trying to find resources for women who work but have no money left after paying their essential bills to also hire a lawyer. I'm sorry to report that there is a void out there. I know women who work two jobs to support themselves and their kids, who have been separated from their husbands for years, but who say they can't afford to get a divorce, and now I am starting to believe them. The filing fees can be waived if a party doesn't have enough money to pay them, but the amount of money a court considers enough is about the same as the amount Legal Aid considers enough. There are special legal foundations to aid special groups in particular. Look for programs for the elderly or the disabled or battered women if you fall into one of those groups. Again, you will be able to get legal help for free because lawyers volunteer their time.

Clinics

Legal clinics, usually associated with law schools, exist in every community with a law school. This is the one bright spot I have found for women who need legal help but can neither afford it privately or qualify for Legal Aid. Different law schools have different programs. Some specialize, just like firms. Most do not. Law students are eager to learn all they can about how to practice law—and they're tired of reading hundreds and hundreds of cases. Just as you will not get inferior medical care at a teaching hospital, like Johns Hopkins or Emory, you will not get inferior legal services from a law school's clinic.

Busted!

You watch television, so you know your Miranda rights. Any time you're arrested, you have the right to remain silent—and you should. Anything you say can—*and will*—be used against you. You have the right to an *attorney*. If you cannot afford one, one will be appointed for you. What if you really can't afford one? You'll be appointed a lawyer. The lawyer might be a public defender, or she might be a private attorney who is appointed by the court to represent you. Most people who work don't qualify for a public defender, so you'll be on your own to hire a lawyer. How do you find one?

Bar associations often have criminal lawyers who hang around the courthouse hoping to get business. As a rule, lawyers can't solicit business in courthouses, but for some reason, bar association lawyers seem to be exempt. Don't hire the first lawyer who flings himself at you if you or someone you care about has been arrested.

How would I find a lawyer if I was busted? I would call the clinic at my law school. They charge fees comparable to the fees charged by private lawyers, but law school criminal lawyers are often of national renown and they come with a handful of eager law students who still believe in the presumption of innocence and are eager to work on a case and impress their nationally renowned teacher.

Stage a Sit-In

One of the greatest resources you have as an American is your access to every branch of government at every level. You can sit in any courtroom in the country. If you're going to be going to court, either by yourself or with a lawyer, you can and should go sit in the same courtroom where you will be heard, and just observe. You'll learn a lot. I still do this. If I'll be appearing in a courtroom that's new to me, I'll watch other cases there beforehand, just to get a feel for how things work in that courtroom. In some places you need to check in. In others you just have a seat and the clerk calls the cases. If you're doing a case *pro se*, you'll want to observe where the parties stand in the courtroom.

You can observe traffic court, criminal court, civil court, and any other kind of court that interests you. Nobody can keep you out because there is a public interest in court proceedings being open to public observation. (The only exception is juvenile court. There is a public interest in keeping juvenile matters private.) If, for example, I am going to do a jury trial, I will try to watch at least part of a jury trial before that same judge, because every judge sets different rules for interviewing potential jurors, for publishing (showing) documents to the jury, etc. Nobody will ask you any questions about who you are or why you are there.

You also have a right to attend public hearings in your community and at other levels of government. If, for example, you are going to apply for a zoning variance for an addition to your home, you have a right to go and listen to someone else's hearing so you will know the procedures and the tenor of the deciding committee. The same applies if you're going to appeal your property tax assessment. Go listen to someone else's appeal. You have a right to be there, and it's the best way to learn what to really expect.

Law School

I know, I know—you just finished reading this book, so why would you want to go to law school? You can be powerful and knowledgeable by practicing the skills and ideas I discussed here. But if reading these chapters has increased your interest in law, it's never too late. Anyone can go to law school. If you have a bachelor's degree, you qualify for law school. There is no such thing as pre-law. In every law school class you will find social science majors, engineering majors, former nurses, current doctors, old folks, young folks. You name it, you will find it there. Women in my class went to law school after rearing families and getting divorces. Several people in my class retired from other careers and decided they had always been interested in the law, so they went back to school in their sixties!

Money shouldn't be a big issue, either. They lend law school students one hundred thousand dollars these days to finance their educations. If you think you might like to go to law school, I wholeheartedly encourage you. Study for the LSAT, or Law School Admissions Test. The score you get after you take it once should give you an idea which schools might be appropriate for you. The LSAT has nothing to do with the law, so don't worry about that, either. It supposedly tests use of language and logic and other silly stuff that is supposed to measure your ability to learn to think like a lawyer.

Law school or not, keep learning everything you can. Take classes. Read books. No one can ever take education away from you—no matter how you acquired it. Knowledge really is power, and you can't be too smart or too powerful.

Good luck!

Index